# BLOSSOMING
## *Embroidery*

### REBEKAH MARSHALL

**Tuva Publishing**
www.tuvapublishing.com

**Adress** Merkez Mah. Cavusbasi Cad. No:71
Cekmekoy - Istanbul 34782 / Türkiye
Tel: 0216 642 62 62

**Blossoming Embroidery**

**First Print** 2024/August

All Global Copyrights Belong to
Tuva Tekstil ve Yayincilik Ltd.

**Content** Embroidery

**Editor in Chief** Ayhan DEMİRPEHLİVAN
**Project Editor** Kader DEMİRPEHLİVAN
**Designer** Rebekah MARSHALL
**Tehnical Editor** Leyla ARAS
**Graphic Designers** Ömer ALP, Abdullah BAYRAKÇI,
Tarık TOKGÖZ, Yunus GÜLDOĞAN

**ISBN** 978-605-7834-82-9

 TuvaYayincilik   TuvaPublishing

 TuvaYayincilik  TuvaPublishing

# Contents

# Projects

# Introduction

Hello my friend! I'm so happy that you've chosen this book, and are looking to step foot into the world of hand embroidery. If you are new to this hobby, you have so much fun coming your way. This craft is slow and therapeutic, but also exciting and very fulfilling. If you are already experienced in embroidery, I'm so glad that you picked up this book, and I hope you are inspired by the patterns it includes.

Hand embroidery itself is very simple, requires very minimal tools, and is perfect for anyone looking for a hands-on craft. I picked up embroidery a few years ago when looking for a hobby and fell in love with it very quickly. It has been both healing, and enjoyable for me, and has opened so many doors throughout the years. Across social media, I have made many friends through this art form, and I am always inspired by the other artists I follow. Florals have always made my heart especially happy, and they are forever my favorite things to stitch.

In this book you will find 15 floral designs inspired by the world around us. These beautiful, blossoming pieces are made with bright, eye-catching color palettes that I hope bring some joy to your heart. These designs were created for all skill levels, and can be customized to fit your own aesthetic. Use these patterns for décor in your own home, or for gifting to a loved one. Any of these designs can also be used to stitch different types projects, like clothing, bags, canvases, etc. Overall, I hope you find enjoyment and fulfillment while stitching these pieces, and that you continue to make beautiful things.

Rebekah Marshall

Bek's Stitches

# Project Gallery

*Blooming Butterfly*
P. 42

*Flying Friend*
P. 46

*Blooms & Mushrooms*
P. 50

*Cactus Blossoms*
P. 54

*Wild Flowers*
P. 58

*Spring Bicycle*
P. 62

*Fruity Florals*
P. 66

*Sunny Bouquet*
P. 70

Fresh Stems
P. 74

Perfect Posies
P. 78

Flower Par-tea
P. 82

Blossoming Love
P. 86

Crescent Blooms
P. 90

Radiant Wreath
P. 94

Floating Florals
P. 98

# Supplies

When it comes to supplies, there are so many different preferences and options out there. It's fun to experiment with types of supplies and materials, so you can decide what you like the most. Here is some useful information, as well as some tips and tricks that you can use when gathering the supplies you'll need to get started.

## Embroidery Threads

Classic six-strand embroidery floss is the most popular type of thread used for embroidery. You can find this sold as skeins in your local craft store. The floss can be separated from six strands into smaller amounts if you'd like to stitch small details or play with texture. You can also find specialty types of embroidery floss as well, such as satin, metallic, wool, and even glow-in-the-dark. Experiment with all of the different types to get a feel for what you prefer to work with. Use as many or as few colors as you like. The designs in this book are stitched with DMC brand embroidery floss, including six-strand embroidery thread, metallic pearl cotton, and Diamant thread. The number codes will be included within the book to make the designs easy to follow.

### Stranded Cotton 25

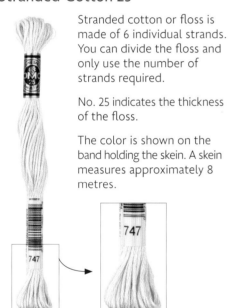

Stranded cotton or floss is made of 6 individual strands. You can divide the floss and only use the number of strands required.

No. 25 indicates the thickness of the floss.

The color is shown on the band holding the skein. A skein measures approximately 8 metres.

747

### Pearl Cotton 5

Thicker than embroidery cotton 25, this thread is twisted and shiny. The strands are indivisible. A skein measures approximately 25 metres.

### Pearl Cotton 8

This thread is thinner than pearl cotton 5 and is sold in a ball.

### Pearl Cotton 12

This thread is thinner than pearl cotton 8.

### PEARL COTTON

This thread is twisted and has a silky, satin-like appearance. There are 4 sizes: 3, 5, 8 and 12. The strands are indivisible. It used as a single thread for embroidery.

### Other Embroidery Threads

A    B    C    D

A: Embroidery floss (stranded cotton)
B: Satin embroidery floss
C: Tapestry wool
D: Diamant metalic thread

A. Made of four indivisible strands that are embroidered as one thread. Comes in different sizes, such as No 16, No 20, No 25, etc.
B. Shiny 100% rayon thread.
C. Thick 100% wool thread.
D. Metalic thread.

### Actual Size

—————————— 1 strand of stranded cotton
—————————— 6 stands of stranded cotton

—————————— 1 strand of pearl cotton 8
—————————— 1 strand of pearl cotton 5

### COLOR CODE

The color code changes from one brand to another. DMC embroidery thread is used in this book.

# Needles

Needles come in different types and size numbers, so it can be a little confusing when you start out. I prefer to use size 24 tapestry (dull-pointed) or chenille (sharp-pointed) needles in my projects, as they have a larger eye and make it easy to thread your needle. Size 5 embroidery needles have a smaller eye and are very sharp, which are good for smaller details. Because it is all about personal preference, look for an assorted pack of needles so that you can try out different sizes and types to see what you prefer while stitching.

## Sharp Pointed Embroidery Needles

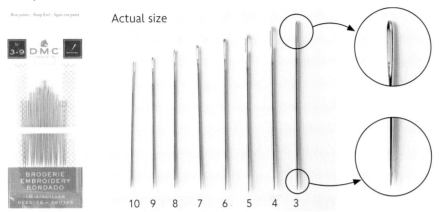

Actual size

10 9 8 7 6 5 4 3

The larger the number, the finer the needle.

Choose needle size to suit the number of strands of thread used.

The difference between sharp and blunt tipped embroidery needles:

> Not only is the point different, but the eye of the needle is larger than needles with a pointed tip.

## Crewel Needle
Actual size

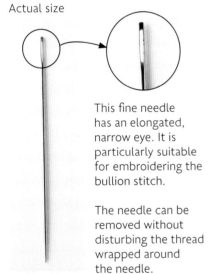

This fine needle has an elongated, narrow eye. It is particularly suitable for embroidering the bullion stitch.

The needle can be removed without disturbing the thread wrapped around the needle.

## Tapestry Needle*
Actual size

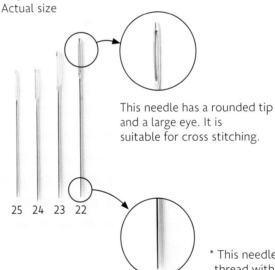

25 24 23 22

This needle has a rounded tip and a large eye. It is suitable for cross stitching.

* This needle is also used to work under a thread without touching the fabric.

## Chenille Needle
Actual size

With its large eye and pointed tip, this needle is suitable for embroidering on dense canvas and with thick thread, such as wool or ribbon.

There are needles to suit each embroidery technique and thickness of the thread.

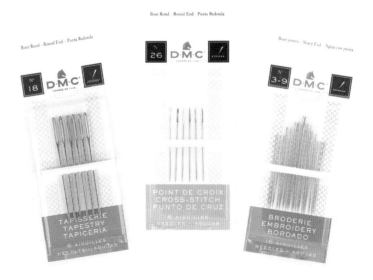

# Fabrics

Fabric comes in all different materials, weaves and colors. The choice is ultimately yours, but for someone starting out, I'd recommend stitching on a non-stretch, 100% cotton fabric. This fabric is easy to prep in your hoop and stays put while you are stitching. Kona Cotton by Robert Kaufman is a very popular fabric amongst stitchers, as it is high quality, thick, and great to stitch on. For more texture, use something with a loose weave, such as linen. Whatever you decide to stitch on can most likely be found in your local craft store. The designs in this book are all stitched on various colors of Robert Kaufman brand fabric (Kona Cotton, and Essex Linen). Feel free to experiment with any color of fabric that you like. Bright, bold colors can make for an exciting background to your design. There are even ways to transfer your pattern onto darker colors, such as sticky water-soluble stabilizer, or white carbon paper.

## Fabric for Traditional Embroidery

Off-white linen fabric

White linen

### THREAD COUNT

The "count" indicates the number of threads per inch (approximately 2.54 cm). The larger the number, the denser the fabric.

## Fabrics for Traditional and Counted-Thread Embroidery

Belfast linen
(25 count)

Cashel linen
(28 count)

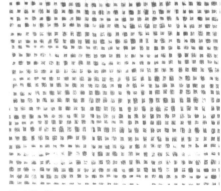

Dublin linen
(25 count)

## Counted-Thread Embroidery Fabrics

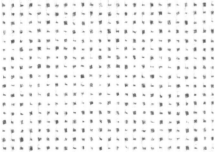

Lugana cotton and viscose
(25 count)

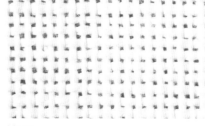

Linen
(20 count)

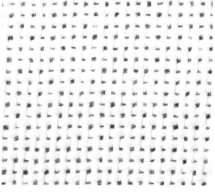

Cotton
(20 count)

13

# Equipment

## Embroidery Hoops

Embroidery hoops also come in several different shapes, sizes, and materials. Classic wood embroidery hoops are best to use when starting out, as they are the most popular and are great at holding your fabric taut. It's important to pay attention to how much tension there is with your hoop, as low tension can lead to puckering of fabric. Certain plastic hoops can also provide great tension and add a fun look to your piece. I love to use high-quality beech wood hoops to frame my pieces, as you will see throughout the book. You can get these online, or you may be able to find them in your local craft store as well.

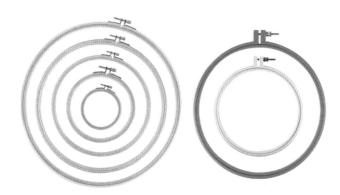

Choose the size according to the item to be embroidered. Hoops with a diameter of 10 cm to 15 cm are practical.

Straight Blade          Curved Blade

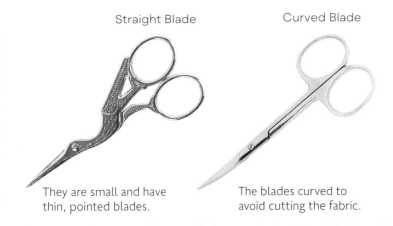

## Embroidery Scissors

It will be very helpful to have two types of scissors on hand while doing embroidery. Use a larger pair of scissors to cut and trim your fabric. Also keep a smaller pair of embroidery scissors with you while stitching so that you can snip thread.

They are small and have thin, pointed blades.

The blades curved to avoid cutting the fabric.

## Pens & Transfer Supplies

I use heat-erase pens to transfer my patterns onto fabric. Once you are done stitching, you can erase the markings using a hair dryer. There are many other options as well, such as water soluble pens/markers, wash-away stabilizers, carbon paper, or just regular pens and pencils. If you are using something non-erasable, be sure to cover up your lines completely with your stitches.

## Carbon Paper

Used to transfer the pattern on to the fabric.

## Tracing Paper

Placed over the pattern to trace it.

## Needle Threader

Used to help thread the needle.

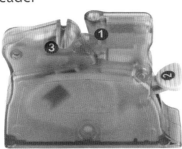

# How To Prep Your Hoop

Start out by cutting yourself a square piece of fabric that is a few inches larger than your hoop. For example, if you are using a 6 inch hoop, a 8.5-10"(22-25,4 cm) piece of fabric will work best. You can transfer your pattern onto the fabric before you put it into your hoop, or once it is already in the hoop. My preferred method is as follows:

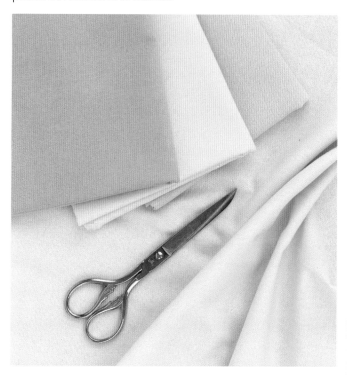

Separate the two pieces of your embroidery hoop. The inner hoop will go first, then place your fabric on top. Next, place your outer hoop over the fabric, and push the two hoops together so that the fabric fits snugly between them. Begin to tighten the screw on your hoop a little, and as you do so, pull your fabric tight. Continue to tighten your screw as you stretch your fabric throughout the hoop. Once your fabric is taut in the hoop, like a drum, finish screwing your hoop as tight as you can get it.

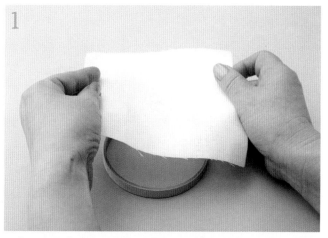

Remove the outer hoop. Place the fabric over the inner hoop, positioning the embroidery pattern in the centre of the hoop.

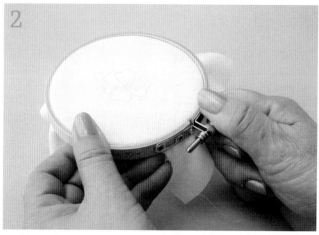

Place the outer hoop over the fabric. Then tighten the screw, while pulling the fabric taut.

With the fabric taut in the hoop, try holding the screw in your non-dominant hand while embroidering to prevent the thread from tangling around it.

Now that your fabric is snug in the hoop, you can continue on to transferring your pattern. I like to flip my hoop, so that the inner hoop is showing, and the fabric is facing the opposite way. Lay your fabric down so that it directly touches the surface you are tracing from. You can copy your pattern directly from this book, by laying the fabric against the design and tracing it. You can also print out a design and use a light source such as a lightbox or a window, or you can pull up a photo of the pattern on a tablet and trace directly from the screen by laying your hoop flat on the surface.

Now that your pattern is traced, you are ready to stitch. You can leave the design in your hoop as is and change it later, or you can unscrew the hoop and flip your fabric around so that the design lines up with the outer hoop.
I tend to stitch my design with the hoop on "backwards" and then flip it once I get towards the end of my stitching.

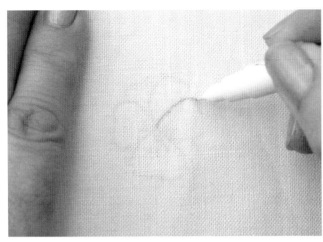

If the fabric is semi-transparent, trace the pattern onto it using a water-erasable fabric marker.

To transfer the pattern onto dark fabric, put carbon paper over the fabric and place the pattern and cellophane on top. Use a stylus to trace the pattern.

Now it is time to prep your needle and thread. Pulling from the numbered end of your skein, cut yourself a length of thread that is comfortable for you to work with. I like to work with a length of 18-36 inches (45,7-91,4 cm) at a time, depending on what I am stitching. Feel free to work with less or more. Experiment with what feels comfortable for you. While I prefer to work with all 6 strands of thread, you can choose to separate your strands and work with fewer. To separate your strands of thread, pull a single strand of thread out, while holding the rest in place with your other hand. It works best to pull your strands out one at a time, and then put them back together when you have the number of strands that you need. Once you have your floss ready, you can thread your needle. Hold your needle in one hand and your floss in the other. Pinching the very end of your thread between your thumb and index finger, wiggle your needle between your fingers as you push the thread through. Pull a few inches of your floss through the eye of the needle. At the other end of your thread, tie a single knot to secure it. You are now ready to begin stitching.

As you stitch, your working thread will become shorter and shorter. When you get to a point where you begin to run out of thread, make sure you end your stitch on the back of your piece. Remove your needle from the thread, and tie the end of your thread in a knot that is snug against the back of your fabric. Trim the excess thread off, then repeat the needle threading process with a new length of floss.

# Thread Preparation

These methods make embroidery thread easier to use.

## Stranded Cotton

This method gives a thread lengths of 100 cm. It is also possible to take the strands one by one and cut them to the desired length.

Remove the labels and set them aside.

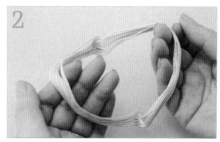

Separate the floss from the centre to form a loop.

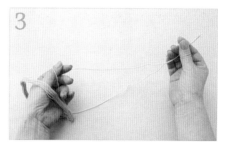

Put one hand in the loop. Keep the loop shape as you unwind it.

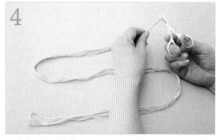

Fold in half three times, then cut at the end. A skein measures approximately 8 metres, so you will obtain 8 lengths of 100cm.

Place 1 label over the 8 lengths. Fold in half and place the other label over the ends of the floss.

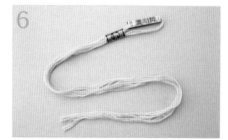

Slide the labels to the middle of the skein. All threads have now been cut to the same length.

## Pearl Cotton 5

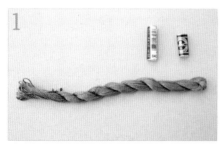

Remove labels.

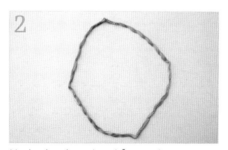

Undo the thread and form a loop.

## Pearl Cotton 8 and 12

The end of the thread is found in the centre.

Cut the knot from the end.

Slip first label over the threads. Fold in half and slide the second label over all the ends.

## Threading Needle

Separate the strands one by one from the middle using a needle.

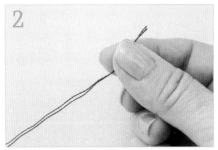

Place the required number of strands together.

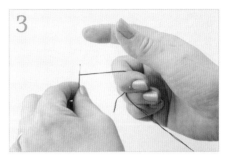

Fold the strands and use a needle to sharpen the fold.

Remove the needle from the fold.

Insert the fold through the eye of the needle.

Pull the folded strands through the eye to thread the needle.

## Using a Needle Threader

To thread a large number of strands or pearl cotton 5, a needle threader is helpful. Insert the tip of the threader through the eye of the needle, then insert the thread in the tip of the needle threader. Pull the tip of needle threader back through the needle.

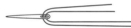

Eye

## Thread Length

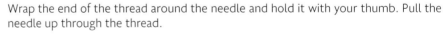

You can use threads of up to 100cm. If that is too long, cut them in half to obtain a length of about 50cm. Thread the needle and fold the thread back by about a third.

## End Knot

Wrap the end of the thread around the needle and hold it with your thumb. Pull the needle up through the thread.

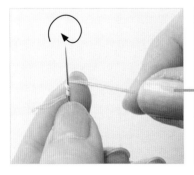 → 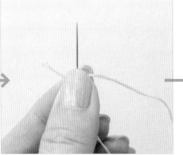 → 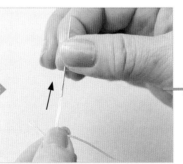 →

Cut the thread close to the knot.

# Starting and Finishing Embroidery

## Outline Stitches

Choose a technique suited the particular style embroidery.

### Start

On the right side of your work, insert the needle a small distance from the start of the pattern. Bring the needle out at the starting point and start embroidering (1).

### Finishing off

Bring the needle out on the wrong side of your work and work it under a few stitches (3). Work back to the last stitch, working under the stitches, then cut the thread next to the stitch (4 and 5).

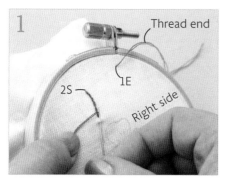

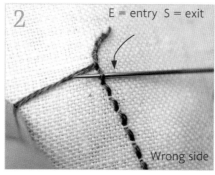

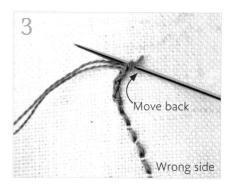

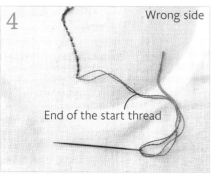

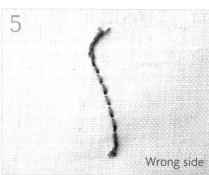

## Filling Stitches

### Start

Sew a few stitches in the part to be filled. Cut the end of the thread close to the fabric (1).
Start embroidering the pattern over the first stitches (2).

### Finishing off

Bring out the needle on the wrong side of the fabric and work the needle under a few stitches (3).
Work back to the last stitch, working under the other stitches, then cut the thread close to the fabric (4 and 5)

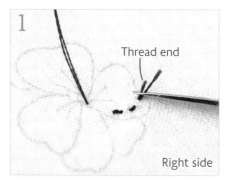

## Knotted Stitches

### Start

Sew a cross over 2 threads of the fabric on the wrong side (1 and 2). Bring out the needle on the right side and make the knot (3).

### Finishing off

Bring out the needle on the wrong side and work it under the starting stitch, then cut the thread (4 and 5).

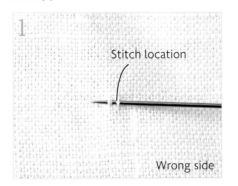

Stitch location

Wrong side

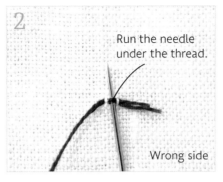

Run the needle under the thread.

Wrong side

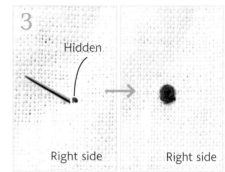

Hidden

Right side

Right side

Wrong side

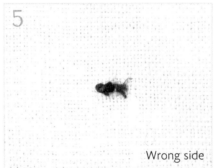

Wrong side

## Start of Additional Stitches

If stitches have already been embroidered in the pattern, work the thread under a few of these stitches. Then return to where this thread should start.

Wrong side

Wrong side

## Embroidery with Double Thread

Fold the thread in half and insert both ends through the eye of the needle. Work the needle under the embroidered stitches, then through the loop formed by the thread.

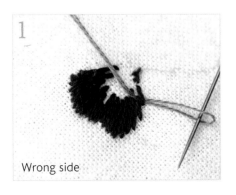

Wrong side

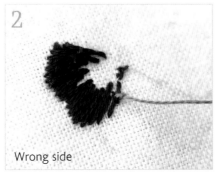

Wrong side

Fold

Thread the 2 ends of the wire.

20

# How To Finish Your Hoop

When you've completed your embroidery piece, you will want to finish the piece off so that it is ready to be displayed. This includes trimming the excess fabric around the edges, and closing off the back if preferred. There are many ways that you can finish off your piece. One of the more traditional ways is the following:

Once finished stitching, remove your fabric and embroidered piece from the hoop. If you would like to cover the backing to protect the stitches, grab a separate piece of fabric. This also gives the finished piece a polished look. I prefer to take a pretty piece of patterned or colorful fabric to put on the back, but you can also finish off with white fabric or with the color you used to stitch on. Place the inner hoop down, and lay the back piece of fabric on top of the hoop. Next, lay down your finished embroidered piece over the backing fabric. Pop your outer hoop back on to the piece, and push the inner and outer hoops together again. Like you did when you prepped your hoop, you will begin to tighten the screw on your hoop as you pull on the edges of your fabric. Continue to tighten your screw as you stretch your fabric throughout the hoop. Make sure you pay attention to both layers of fabric, and that you are getting both pieces nice and tight. Once your fabric is taut in the hoop, like a drum, finish screwing your hoop as tight as you can get it.

Trim the back layer of fabric down all the way to the hoop using your fabric scissors. With your scissors, you will now trim the embroidery piece's fabric down to about a 1-2" (2,5-5 cm) circle. Thread your needle again with a piece of floss that is about the length of the circumference of your hoop. Coming up from the back of your fabric, near the top of the hoop, use a running stitch to begin stitching the fabric closed. This will start to create a ruffle effect as your stitch your way around the circle. When you get all the way around to the end, you will want to end with your needle and thread going down into the back of the fabric again. Remove your needle from the thread. Take both ends of floss in your hands and pull the ruffled fabric so that it is closed tight around the back of the hoop. Tie both ends together in a knot, and trim the excess thread. When you flip  your hoop back around, you should not be able to see any of the excess fabric anymore. Now your piece is properly framed and ready to be displayed.

# Tips for Obtaining a Neat Finish

## 1 Pattern Transfer

Iron the fabric, straightening the weave before transferring the pattern. Try to draw the lines of the pattern in one go time to avoid overlapping lines. Follow a straight thread in the weave when drawing straight lines. Using a circle template allows you to obtain precise circles.

Divide the circle equally and put the marks.

Draw a circle using a compass.

## 2 Correct Needle

Choose the size of the needle according to the number of strands. A fine needle is suitable for embroidering with 1 strand. A needle with a sufficiently large eye is recommended for embroidering with more than 2 strands. Choose a large needle to embroider on a thick fabric.

## 3 Regular Thread Tension

Take care to obtain a regular thread tension. If the thread is too tight, the fabric may pucker. On the other hand, if the thread is too loose, the stitches may "detach" from the fabric.

## 4 Holding The Thread

When embroidering, lightly hold the thread with the thumb of your left hand. This helps regulate the tension of the thread and prevents tangling.

## 5

When embroidering, the thread tends to twist. Untwist the thread to avoid tangling and sew uniform stitches.

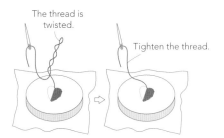

The thread is twisted.

Tighten the thread.

## 6 Pilling

The thread often pills as a result of friction against the fabric. It is advisable to change the thread if you undo stitches or you notice pilling.

## 7 Small Stitches in Curves

Embroider curves with smaller stitches so that they look as natural as possible.

Embroider with small stitches.

## 8 Wrong Side of The Fabric

It is possible to carry the thread on the wrong side of the fabric to embroider nearby motifs. However, if they are more than 2 cm apart, fasten off the thread at the end of each motif.

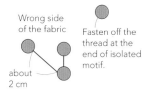

Wrong side of the fabric

Fasten off the thread at the end of isolated motif.

about 2 cm

# Finishing Touches and Care

## Finishing Touches

When you have finished your embroidery, check the stitches have been properly fastened off on the wrong side of the fabric. Then erase the fabric marker.

Spray water or dab the pattern with a moisten cotton bud to erase the water erasable marker.

Allow it dry completely, then iron. If the fabric is still wet, the marker lines may reappear and become permanent.

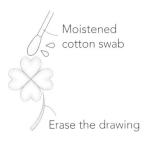

Moistened cotton swab

Erase the drawing

## Ironing

Place a towel on the ironing board and iron the item on the wrong side at a temperature suitable for the fabric.

## Washing

Hand wash with neutral detergent. Gently squeeze out water and lay fabric flat. Allow to dry in the shade.

# Embroidery Stitch Guide

## STRAIGHT STITCH

Bring your needle up through the fabric at one point, then down through the fabric at the next point forming one straight stitch.

Simply embroider straight stitches. The length and direction of this stitch may vary.

Actual size

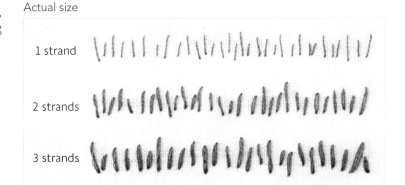

1 strand

2 strands

3 strands

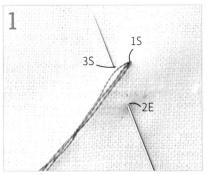

**1**

Bring your needle out at 1S, and insert again at 2E. Bring the needle out at 3S to complete your first stitch.

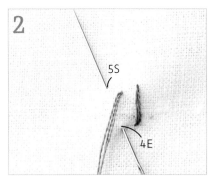

**2**

Insert your needle at 4E, then bring back out at 5S.

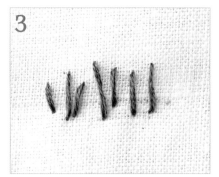

**3**

Repeat this process to complete your straight stitches.

## SEED STITCH

Create this stitch by scattering short, straight stitches in several different directions, like scattered seeds.

These little stitches are like seeds. Embroider them stitch by stitch like the back stitch. They are embroidered in all directions to fill an area.

Actual size (3 strands)

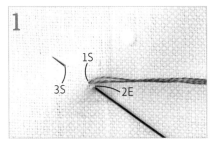

**1**

Bring your needle out at 1S, and insert again at 2E. Bring the needle out at 3S to complete your first stitch.

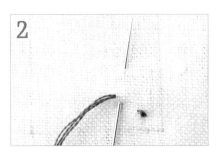

**2**

Seed stitches are similar to small straight stitches.

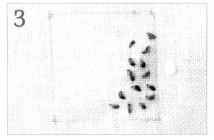

**3**

Embroider multiple stitches in various directions to fill your area with seed-like stitches.

# BACK STITCH

Coming up through from the back of your fabric, make a single stitch as long or as short as you'd like. Continue down the line you are following, leaving space between your last stitch and your current one. Bring your needle up through the fabric, then back down through the second point from your first stitch. Repeat this for as long as needed. Tip: If you are trying to stitch a round shape, it will help to use smaller stitches.

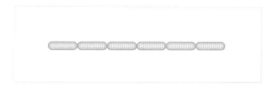

Actual size

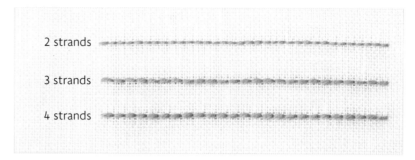

2 strands

3 strands

4 strands

This stitch can create a continuous line. It is embroidered backwards towards the previous stitch.

※ Working direction ⟵

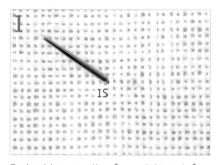

Embroider your line from right to left. Bring your needle up at 1S, about one stitch-length away from the line's starting point.

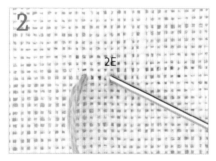

Bring your needle back down at 2E (the line's starting point).

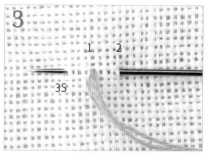

Bring your needle up again at 3S, about one stitch-length away from 1S.

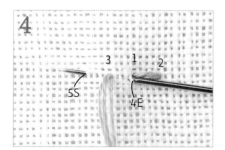

Pull your thread through, then insert your needle at 4E. Bring your needle up at 5S.

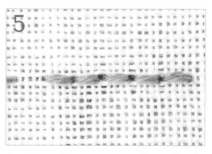

Continue this process until your line is fully stitched.

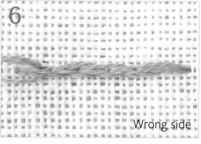

View from the back—the reverse side will look like a split back stitch.

# WHIPPED BACK STITCH

Create a basic back stitch line. Next, bring your needle back up through the end point of your back stitch line. Weave your thread under each stitch starting from the right, going under to the left, then back up and over to the next stitch. Continue weaving under each stitch, then bring your needle back down through the very first point.

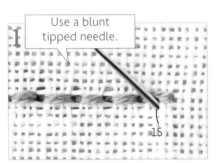

Run the thread in a downward direction under the back stitches.

Actual size (3 strands for the back stitch and 2 strands of contrast color)

※ Working direction ←

Use a blunt tipped needle.

Create your back stitch line.
Next, bring your needle up at 1S (underneath your first back stitch).

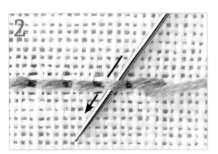

Weave your needle under the next stitch in a downward direction.

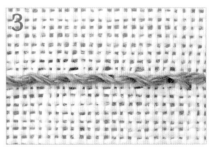

Continue this technique, weaving under each stitch. Do not insert your needle into the fabric until the end.

# SPLIT BACK STITCH

Coming up from the back of your fabric, make a single stitch. Bring your needle back up, about half of a stitch-length away from the previous stitch. As you make your next stitch, bring your needle down through the thread of the previous stitch, splitting it through the middle. This will make an almost chain-like effect with your thread. Continue on until your line is finished.

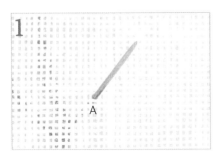

Bring your needle up at point A.

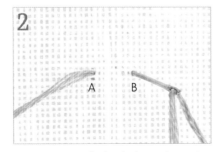

Bring your needle back down through point B to create your first stitch.

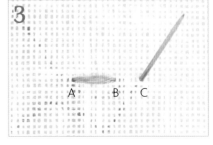

Bring your needle up again at point C (about half of a stitch-length away from your previous stitch).

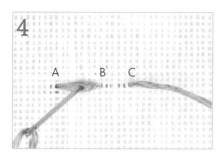

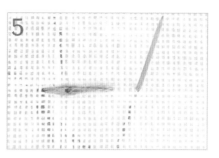

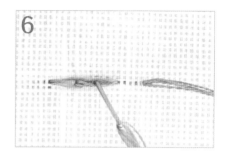

As you bring your needle back down, split the previous stitch with your needle.

Continue this process until your line is finished.

Your split back stitch will appear similar to a chain stitch.

## BRICK STITCH

Using a back stitch technique, layer rows of this stitch in a brick formation.

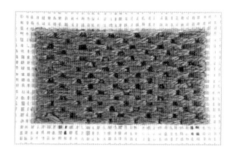

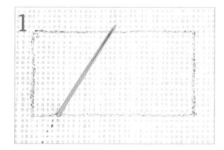

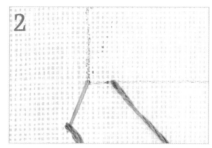

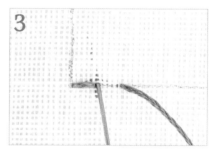

Bring your needle up about one stitch-length away from the line's starting point.

Bring your needle back down at the line's starting point, creating your first stitch.

Continue this process, creating a simple back stitch line.

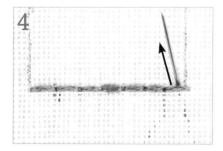

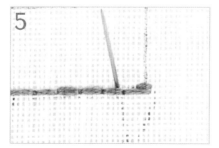

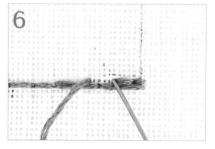

As you continue on to your next row, bring your needle up in the center, above your last stitch on the first row. Bring it back down at the end point to create a half-stitch.

Bring your needle up again above the center of the stitch below. Create another back stitch.

Continue this process, creating staggering, brick-like patterns of stitches.

# FISHBONE STITCH

If you are using this stitch for a leaf, make a straight stitch from the tip of your shape, about a third of the way down. Following the outer line of your shape, make another stitch next to original stitch, bringing it diagonally down below the first stitch, barely crossing over. Come in from the opposite side, into the middle again, overlapping the previous stitch. Continue repeating these stitches, switching sides each time. You will get an overlapping fishbone effect that makes the perfect texture for leaves.

The appearance of this stitch is reminiscent of fish bones. It is often used to embroider leaves.

Actual size (3 strands)

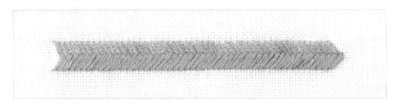

※ Working direction (embroider vertically) →

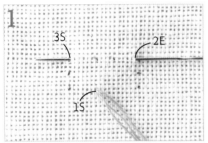

Bring your needle up through the fabric at 1S. Come back through at 2E, then out again at 3S.

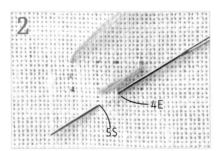

Insert your needle at 4E, pulling back through at 5S.

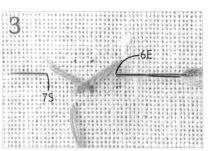

Your stitches will be crossed at the bottom. Continue by bringing your needle down at 6E, then back up at 7S.

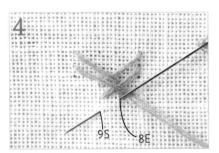

Pull your thread through, then bring your needle down at 8E and up at 9S.

Continue this process as you make your way to the bottom of your shape.

Your fishbone stitch is complete.

## Leaves Embroidered with Fishbone Stitch

### Tight Fishbone Stitch

※ Working direction

### Spaced Fishbone Stitch

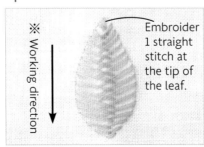

※ Working direction

Embroider 1 straight stitch at the tip of the leaf.

Embroider one straight stitch at the tip of your leaf. Keep your stitches close together to fill the entire surface or space out your stitches to create a ribbed look.

# LAZY DAISY STITCH

Pull your needle through fabric at the middle point. Loop the thread (using your finger can help with this), then bring your needle back through the same hole or right next to it. Do not pull your thread all the way through, leaving the loop you've created. Pull your needle through your fabric again, this time above your first point, being sure to come through the inside of the loop you've made. Bring your needle and thread around the loop and come back down through the same hole. Repeat these steps, coming from the same point in the middle each time you start a new loop. This will make a lazy daisy flower.

This stitch is often used to embroider petals. Work in a circle to create a flower shape.

Actual size

2 strands        3 strands        4 strands

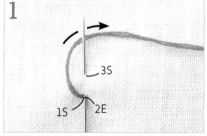

**1** Bring your needle up through the fabric at 1S, then back down through 2E (this will be the same, or very close to the same point). Bring your needle back up at 3S. Wrap your thread around the needle to create a loop.

**2** Pull your thread through, and adjust loop to the size and width you would like it.

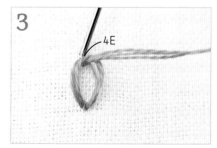

**3** Bring your needle back down at 4E, on the outside of the loop. This stitch anchors your loop to the fabric.

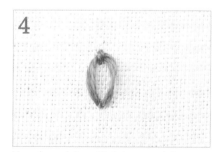

**4** Your lazy daisy stitch is complete.

# CHAIN STITCH

Create one single loop with your needle and thread, as though you are making a single lazy daisy stitch. Pull your needle through your fabric again, this time above your first point, being sure to come through the inside of the loop you've made. Bring your needle and thread back down through the same point, within your loop, to create a new loop while anchoring down the first loop. Repeat this technique to make a chain of stitches, each anchoring the last down. To end your chain, anchor the last loop down the same way you would with a lazy daisy stitch.

This stitch looks like a chain and can be used to create thick lines.
It is important to embroider stitches of a uniform size.

Actual size

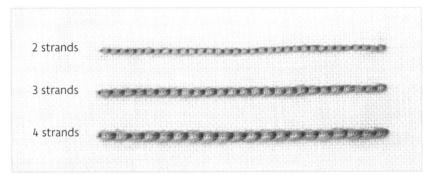

2 strands

3 strands

4 strands

※ Working direction
(embroider vertically)

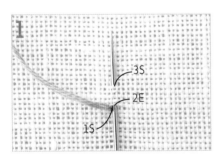

Bring your needle up through the fabric at 1S, then back down through 2E (this will be the same, or very close to the same point). Come back up through the point 3S.

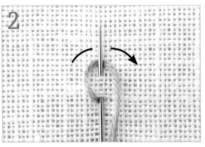

Wrap your thread around and under the needle from left to right to create a loop.

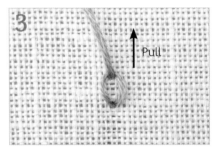

Pull your thread through gently to tighten your chain.

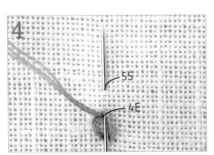

Bring your needle back down at point 4E (same point as 3S), then come back up at 5S.

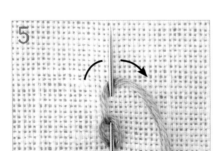

Wrap your thread around and under the needle from left to right to create another loop.

Pull your thread through, and repeat this process until you have a chain-stitched line.

## End

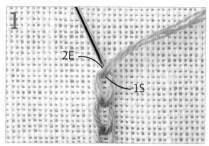

Bring your needle up inside of your final loop. Create a single stitch over the loop to finish it off and anchor it down to your fabric.

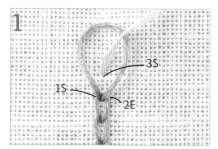

Your chain stitch is complete.

## Adding a Thread

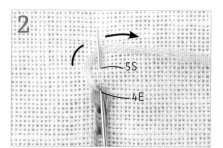

Form a large loop using your original blue thread. Come up at point 3S with your new color.

Pull your blue thread to adjust your loop. Bring the new color back down at 4E, then back up at 5S. Wrap this thread around the needle to create your loop.

Continue embroidering with your new color.

## Chain Stitch Circle

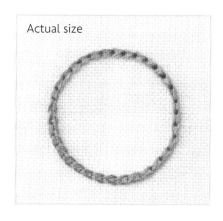

Actual size

Use the chain stitch technique to create a circle shape. As you reach the end of your circle, you can adjust the size of your stitches to ensure they are uniform, and prepare to close the circle.

On your last stitch, run your needle under the loop you created with your first stitch.

To complete the final loop, bring your needle down into the same point you brought it up at.

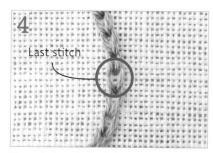

Your chain stitch circle is complete.

# REVERSE CHAIN STITCH

Create one single lazy daisy stitch. Start a new loop below your finished, closed loop. Push your needle between the loop and the fabric, forming a chain, then come back down at your same point. Repeat this process to create a reverse chain stitch. I prefer the reverse chain stitch to the regular chain stitch. Both will give you very similar looks.

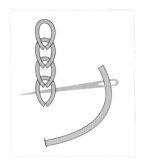

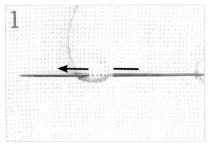

**1** Begin to create a single chain/lazy daisy stitch by bringing your needle up and back down at the same point. Bring your needle up again where you would like the end of your chain to be. Wrap your thread around the needle to create a loop.

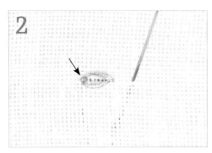

**2** Pull your thread through, and adjust loop to the size and width you would like it. Bring your needle down on the outside of the loop to attach it to your fabric.

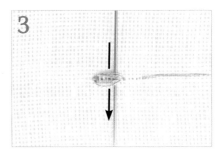

**3** Start your next chain to the right of your first. Run your needle under your first chain.

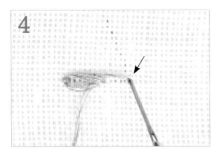

**4** Pull your thread through, then bring your needle back down at your starting point.

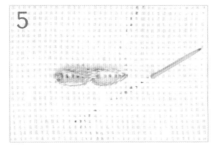

**5** Repeat this process, starting your next chain to the right of your last stitch.

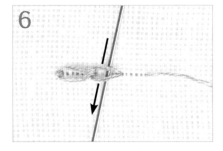

**6** Run your needle under the previous chain.

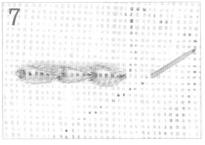

**7** Repeat this process for as long as you would like your chain to be.

# STEM STITCH

Make a single stitch along your line. Bring your needle back through the fabric from underneath the original stitch, however, do not come up through your existing stitch. Instead bring your needle and thread out from the side of the original stitch. Then make the same size stitch, and repeat by bringing your needle up through the fabric from below the second stitch. Continue until your line is finished. This stitch can be used for stems, vines, outlining, etc.

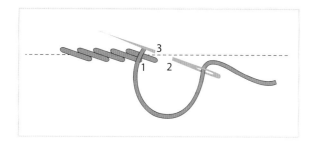

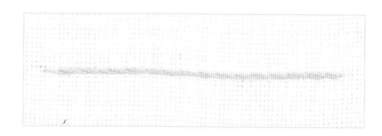

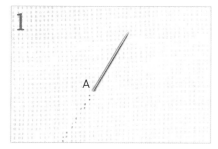

Begin by bringing your needle up at point A, the beginning of your line.

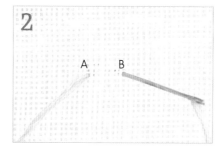

Bring your needle down at point B, but do not pull tight. Leave a small loop of thread.

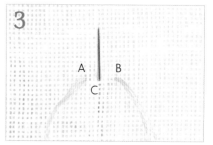

Bring your needle up at point C, and pull the thread all the way through to tighten.

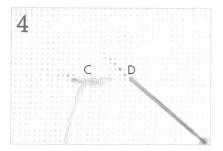

Bring your needle down at point D.

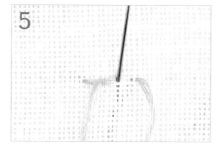

Repeat this process until your stem stitch line is complete.

# FRENCH KNOT

Bring your needle through your fabric in the spot you would like your knot to be. Wrap your thread around the needle, then insert your needle back into the same hole, or right next to the hole. Slowly pull your needle and thread through, while keeping tension with the knotted thread. Pull your knot tight. For an even knot, wrap your thread just once or twice. For more uneven, textured, or larger knots, I will wrap my thread 3, or sometimes 4 times. Play with the tension and speed until you get your technique down.

This stitch forms a small knot.
The knot size depends the number of strands and wraps.

Actual size (the thread has been wrapped twice times around the needle)

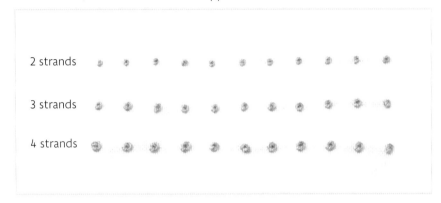

2 strands

3 strands

4 strands

## Thread Wrapped Twice

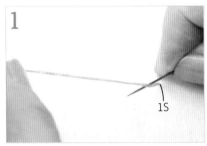

**1**

1S

Bring your needle up at 1S, and hold the thread in your nondominant hand.

**2**

Wrap the thread around your needle two times.

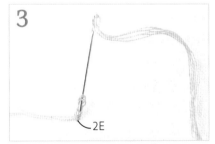

**3**

2E

Insert your needle into the fabric at 2E (the same point or very close to 1S).

**4**

Wrong side

View on the back of your hoop as you pass the needle through your fingers.

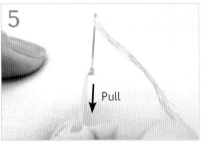

**5**

Pull

Continue to hold your thread with your nondominant hand as you pull the needle through.

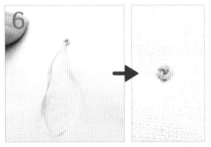

**6**

Pull your needle completely through to form your knot. Your French knot is complete.

## Thread Loosely Wrapped Twice

Actual size

3 strands

## Thread Wrapped Once

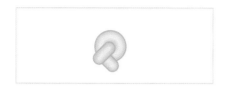

Actual size

3 strands

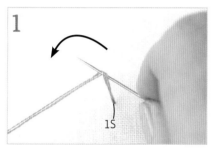

1

Bring your needle up at 1S, and hold the thread with your nondominant hand. Wrap the thread around your needle one time.

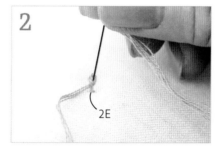

2

2E

Insert your needle into the fabric at 2E (the same point or very close to 1S).

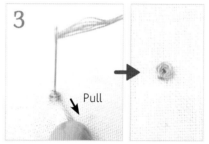

3

Pull

Continue holding onto the thread while pulling your needle through to form the knot.

# SATIN STITCH

Bring your needle up at the edge of the shape you would like to fill, pull your thread across the shape, then through the fabric on the opposite edge. Continue this until your shape is filled. Keeping the perfect tension and same direction while filling in your shape should help your thread look straight and smooth. Though it seems simple, practice makes perfect with this stitch. Experiment with tension, strands of thread, and different shapes. Give yourself a clear outline, and draw some lines through your shape as a guide to help you.

Actual size

Work the thread from one edge to the other of a shape to fill the entire area.

2 strands

3 strands

## Embroider from the centre to the edge.

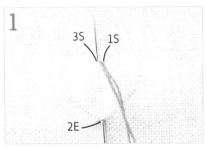

**1** Make one stitch in the middle of your shape from 1S to 2E. Bring your needle back up at 3S.

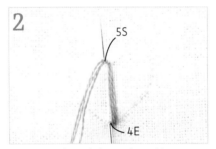

**2** Pull your thread through and insert your needle again at 4E. Bring your needle up at 5S, and continue this pattern of stitching without leaving any space between your stitches.

**3** Half of your shape has been filled with satin stitch.

**4** Return to the center again, and create a stitch next to the initial stitch down the middle (1S).

**5** Continue stitching the other half of your shape.

**6** Your shape has been stitched completely.

# LONG AND SHORT STITCH

Use various lengths of straight stitches, both long and short, to fill in an area. Start at one side of the shape and work your way over to the other. Your stitches will likely overlap and blend together. This is more of a free style stitch that allows you to fill in larger areas with thread.

This stitch can fill a larger area than the satin stitch. It is alternately embroidered with long and short stitches. This stitch can create a nuanced color gradient.

Actual size

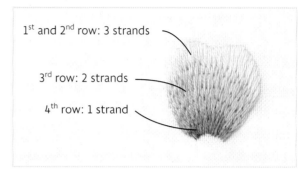

1st and 2nd row: 3 strands

3rd row: 2 strands

4th row: 1 strand

## Embroidered pattern over four rows

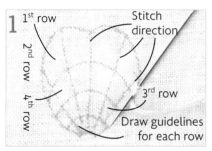

1  1st row
2nd row
4th row
3rd row
Stitch direction
Draw guidelines for each row

Draw guidelines for each row that you will stitch.

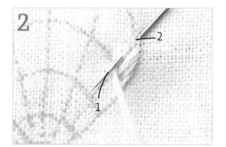

2

Bring your needle up through the fabric at 1, inside of your guidelines. Bring your needle back down at 2, outside of your guidelines.

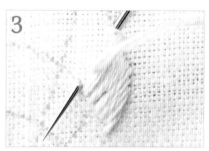

3

Embroider long and short stitches, following the guidelines in your shape. The shorter stitches will be about two thirds the length of your longest stitches.

4

The first row of your shape is complete.

5

Begin to stitch your second row within the guidelines.

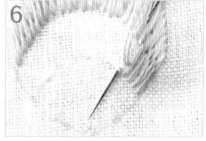

6

In the second row, start each stitch at the end point of the stitches in the first row, stitching into the gaps that appear between the long stitches. You will embroider stitches of equal length, but this technique will make them look like different lengths.

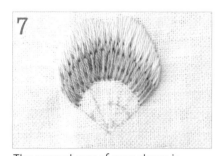

7

The second row of your shape is complete.

8

Stitch your third row using the same technique, using two strands of thread. Stitch the fourth row, and end your stitches at the guideline you've drawn.

# WOVEN ROSE

It helps to begin by drawing a circle as big as you'd like your rose to be. For a small-medium sized rose, make 5 stitches coming from the center to the edge of your circle. This should look like a wagon wheel or a star. Bring your needle through the fabric right near the center of your circle, in between two of the stitches. You will now begin to weave your rose. Pull your needle under the first line, over the second line, under the third, over the fourth, and under the fifth. The amount of tension you use when pulling your needle through will decide how tight and neat or loose and fluffy your rose will look. Work your way around the circle, filling your rose to the edges, covering all of your lines, weaving over and under. When your rose is done, bring your needle back through the fabric somewhere along the other edge of your rose.

Use 12 strands in your larger roses for a fluffier, fuller look. Work slowly and carefully in order to avoid snagging the thread. You can also use 7 spokes to give yourself more control and a tighter weave. Leave an open space in the middle of your and weave around it in order to add French knots or other texture in the middle.

Embroider a star with an odd number of legs, then work the thread above / below each leg to make a pattern resembling the spider web.

Actual size (3 strands)

## A : Legs embroidered with straight stitches

※ Work counter-clockwise.

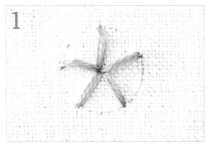

Make five straight stitches (spokes) toward the center to create a star.

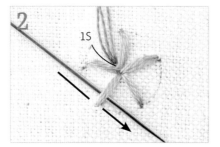

Bring your needle up near the center, between two of your spokes (1S). Weave the needle over and under each of the spokes, alternating as you go.

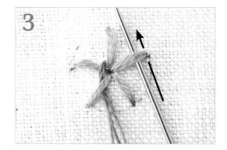

Your first round is complete.

Continue weaving your thread over and under the spokes.

Weave your thread until the spokes are no longer visible. Bring your needle back down into the fabric at 2E.

Your woven rose is complete.

# BASKET WEAVE STITCH

Start by stitching several vertical stitches, all parallel and evenly spaced from one another. Coming up from the side of your vertical stitches, begin to weave horizontally over and under, like you are weaving a basket. Once you reach the other end of your vertical stitches, bring your thread back down. Repeat this step, but this time switch the over/under technique, so that your weaving becomes checkered, like a traditional basket weave. Continue this technique all the way down until your shape is fully woven.

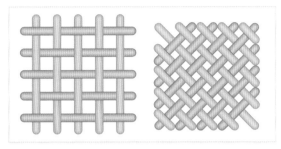

Work the thread above / below each vertical stitch to make a pattern that looks like a weave. The stitch is raised from the fabric.

Actual size (3 strands)

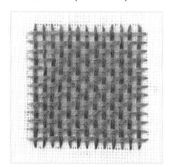

※ There is a gap between the stitch and the fabric.

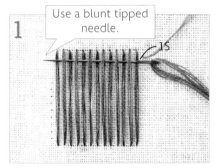

Create a row of long, vertical stitches equal in length. Bring your thread back up at 1S, and begin to weave over and under each of your vertical stitches.

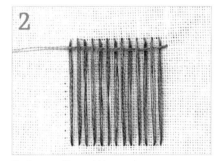

Pull your thread through.

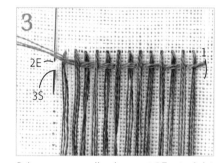

Bring your needle down at 2E, straight across from 1S. Next, bring your needle back up at 3S.

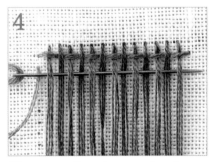

Weave your thread over and under your vertical stitches, opposite to the way you completed the first row (for example, instead of over/under/over, weave under/over/under).

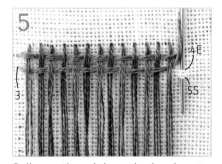

Pull your thread through, then insert your needle back through the fabric at 4E. Bring your needle up at 5S.

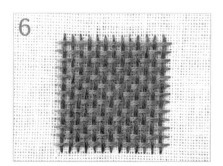

Repeat these steps as you move down in order to create a true woven stitch.

Projects

# BLOOMING
## *Butterfly*

Dive into the world of embroidery with this playful pattern, where nature's beauty meets fluttering charm. This sweet butterfly has a wing stitched with the beauty of blooming florals.

**STEP 1:** Begin by stitching the body of the butterfly using long, vertical satin stitches. You can also stitch the antennas now using two straight stitches.

**STEP 2:** Next, begin to outline the left side of your butterfy using a simple back stitch. You will fill in the black areas of the butterfly using long and short stitches. The colored part of the wings will be filled in using satin stitch. Add in your white dot details using French knots.

**STEP 3:** The right side of your butterfly contains florals stitched with various stitches. For the rose, use your 12-strand woven rose technique. The 3 petaled flowers will be stitched using satin stitch, then filled with French knots in the centers. The looped daisy flowers are stitched using a simple lazy daisy stitch. You will also use this stitch, along with a back stitch, to create the two green, leafy vines. Lastly, use back stitch to stitch your remaining stem, and fishbone to stitch up all of the remaining leaves.

MATERIALS | **Fabric:** Kona Cotton, Ice Peach, K001-1176, 100% cotton, 9x9" (22.6x22.6 cm) square
**Thread:** DMC Mouline Six-Strand Cotton, Colors – 19, 310, 369, 722, 760, 987, 3688, Blanc
**Needle:** DMC Chenille, size 24
**Equipments:** 6" (15 cm) Beechwood Hoop, Scissors, Heat - erase pen

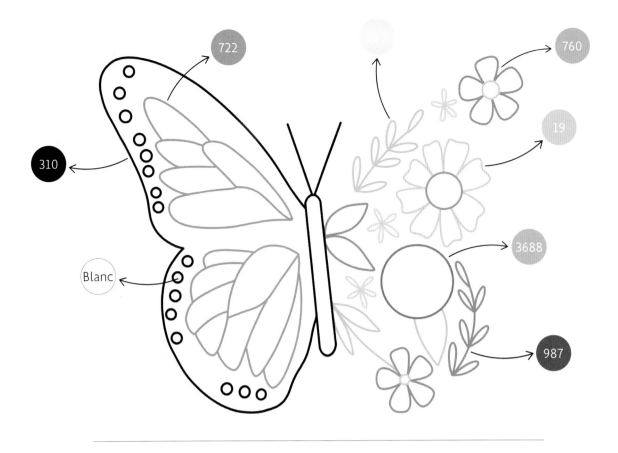

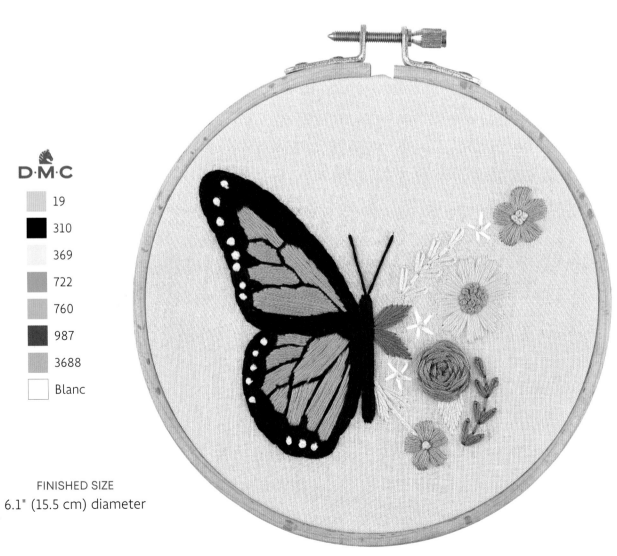

**D·M·C**

- 19
- 310
- 369
- 722
- 760
- 987
- 3688
- Blanc

FINISHED SIZE
6.1" (15.5 cm) diameter

# FLYING
## *Friend*

Let your imagination take flight into a garden of beauty! This charming embroidery pattern captures the grace of a hummingbird in mid-flight, weaving through lush floral branches.

**STEP 1:** Using satin stitch, stitch all of the petals on the flowers throughout the branches. Use different shades of colors to create depth. Fill the center of each flower with a French knot.

**STEP 2:** Stitch your branches using a simple back stitch, and your leaves using fishbone stitch.

**STEP 3:** For your hummingbird, use a combination or long and short stitches, as well as satin stitch to create the body, head, wings, and beak. This will give your bird a feather-type look.

MATERIALS | **Fabric:** Kona Cotton, Sky, K001-1513, 100% cotton, 9x9" (22.6x22.6 cm) square
**Thread:** DMC Mouline Six-Strand Cotton, Colors – 310, 369, 727, 818, 899, 3326, 3350, 3814, Ecru
**Needle:** DMC Chenille, size 24
**Equipments:** 6" (15 cm) Beechwood Hoop, Scissors, Heat-erase pen

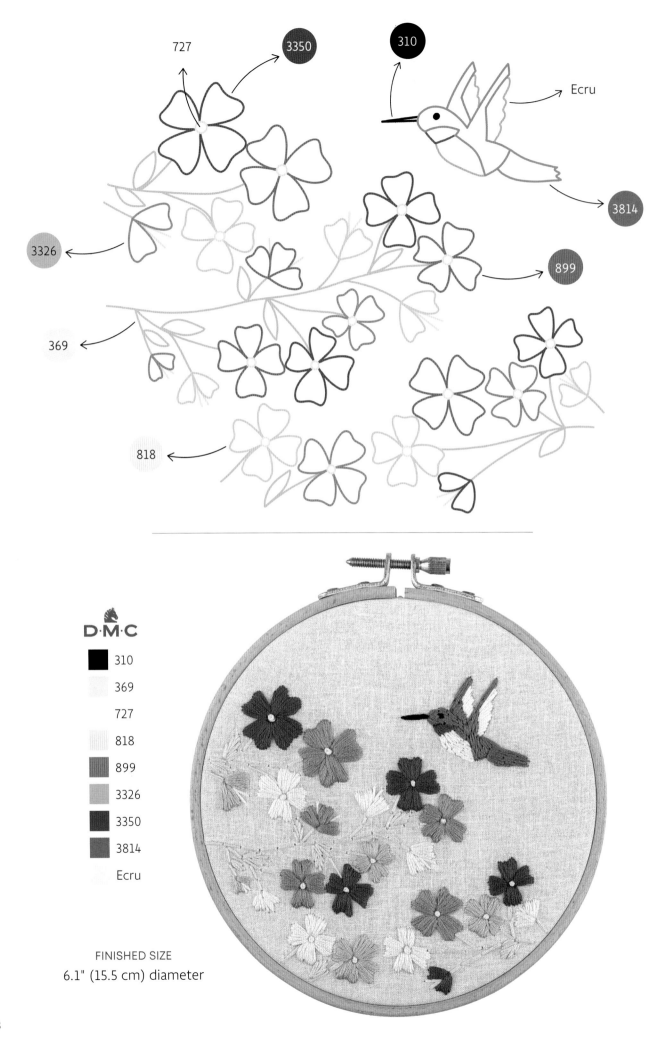

727

3350

310

Ecru

3326

3814

369

899

818

**D·M·C**

310
369
727
818
899
3326
3350
3814
Ecru

FINISHED SIZE
6.1" (15.5 cm) diameter

# BLOOMS & *Mushrooms*

Transform your space with this embroidery pattern that features
a scene where mushrooms are surrounded by a variety of flowers,
poms, and a touch of shimmer.

**STEP 1:** Begin your piece by stitching your mushrooms. These are stitched mainly using satin stitch, but also use back stitch on the large mushroom, and French knots on the two medium sized mushrooms for their spots. Pay attention to the direction your satin stitch goes.

**STEP 2:** Stitch the stems of yours flowers using a stem stitch. Next, stitch your leaves using a fishbone stitch. These leaves have an elongated look, that can be achieved by using longer stitches for the fishbone. For your daisies, use satin stitch for the petals, then fill in the centers with French knots. The circular flowers are made by outlining, then filling in with French knots.

**STEP 3:** Add your finishing touches with scattered metallic French knots and straight stitch sparkles.

MATERIALS | **Fabric:** Kona Cotton, Pearl Pink, K001-1283, 100% cotton, 9x9" (22.6x22.6 cm) square
**Thread:** DMC Mouline Six-Strand Cotton, Colors – 19, 326, 349, 520, 523, 739, 815, 3326, 3832, Blanc, Diamant Color – D3821
**Needle:** DMC Chenille, size 24; DMC Embroidery, size 5
**Equipments:** 6" (15 cm) Beechwood Hoop, Scissors, Heat-erase pen

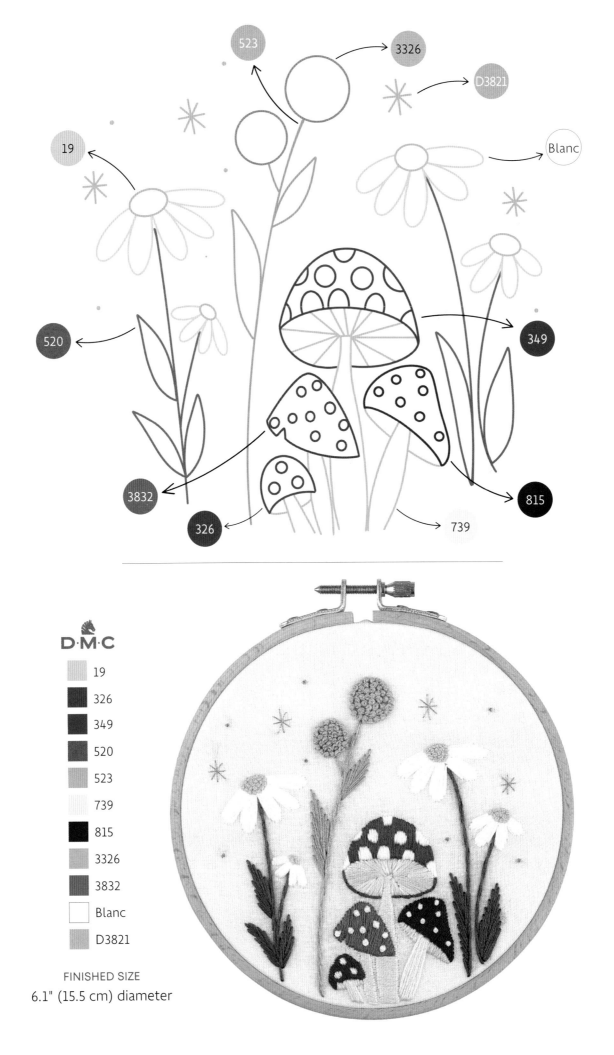

523
3326
D3821
19
Blanc
520
349
3832
815
326
739

**D·M·C**

19
326
349
520
523
739
815
3326
3832
Blanc
D3821

FINISHED SIZE
6.1" (15.5 cm) diameter

# CACTUS *Blossoms*

Immerse yourself in a desert daydream! Combining the prickly beauty of cacti with the delicate radiance of florals, you can design this vibrant and imaginative scene. Let your imagination bloom amidst the desert sands!

**STEP 1:** Start this piece by stitching your dark green cactus using satin stitch for each section. Add your "spikes" by scattering straight stitches in a lighter color. Add the small pink floral detail using three lazy daisy stitches. Complete your aloe-style cactus by using satin stitch as well.

**STEP 2:** Next, stitch the large center cactus. You will outline, then fill with rows of split stitch. Leave spaces for the overlapping flower petals and work around the other cacti that overlap. You will also stitch the small, oval cactus on the left using this same split stitch technique.

**STEP 3:** Move on to the florals, starting with your satin stitch petals. Add details to these flowers using straight stitch, then fill your centers with French knots of various sizes. Next, complete your roses using the woven-rose stitch. For the larger roses, use 12 strands of floss for a thicker, fluffy look. Add your leaves throughout the piece using fishbone stitch.

**STEP 4:** Create your sandy ground by using a seed stitch in a beige color.

MATERIALS | **Fabric:** Kona Cotton, Sand, K001-1323, 100% cotton, 9x9" (22.6x22.6 cm) square
**Thread:** DMC Mouline Six-Strand Cotton, Colors – 19, 437, 469, 602, 702, 704, 727, 776, 890, 893
**Needle:** DMC Chenille, size 24
**Equipments:** 6" (15 cm) Beechwood Hoop, Scissors, Heat-erase pen

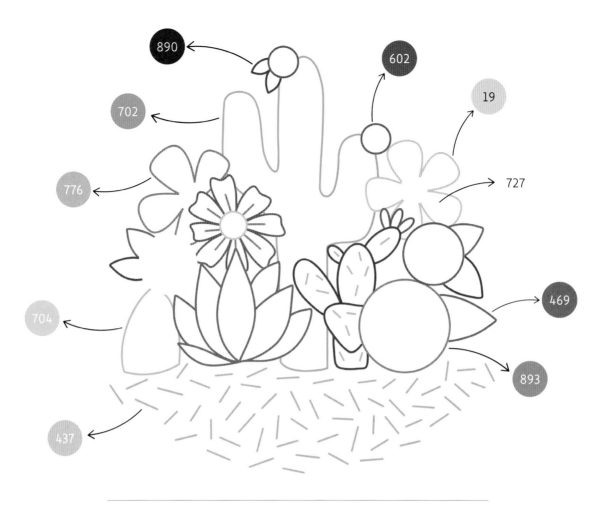

890

602

19

702

776

727

704

469

893

437

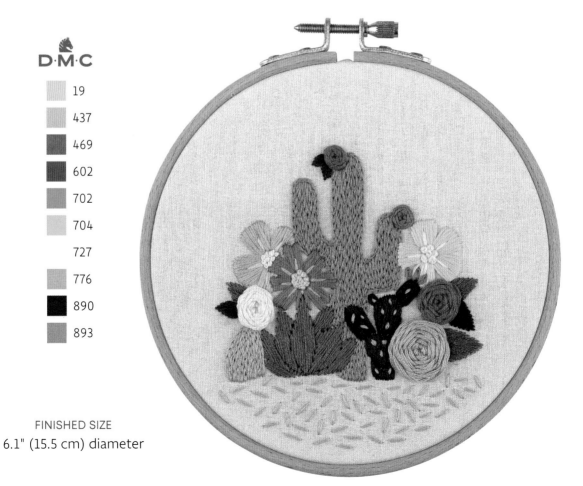

**D·M·C**

19

437

469

602

702

704

727

776

890

893

FINISHED SIZE
6.1" (15.5 cm) diameter

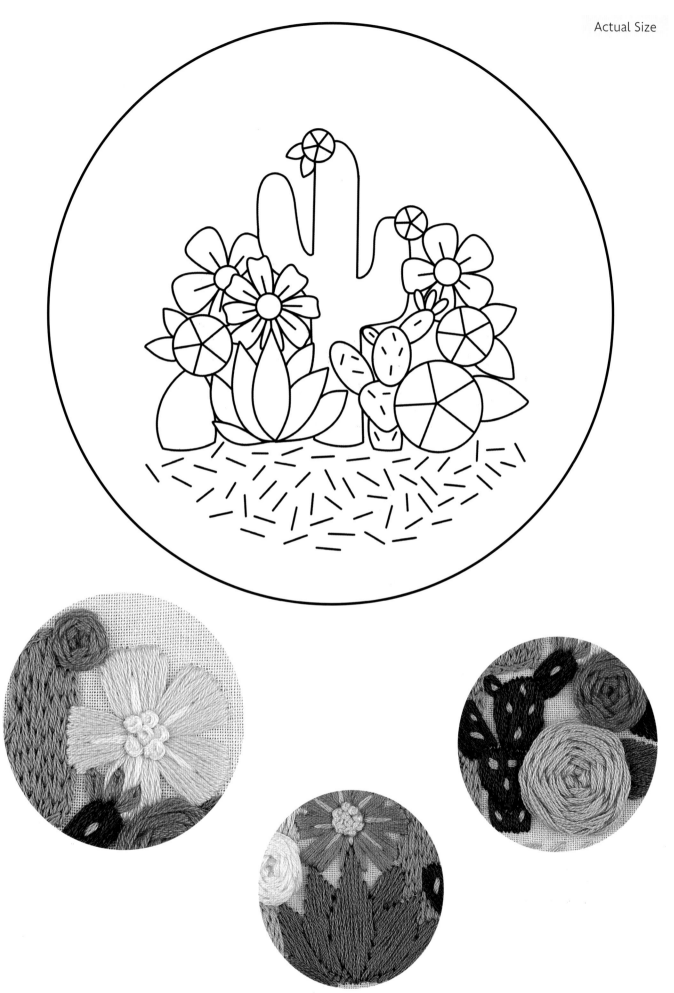

# WILD
## *Flowers*

This adorable design features a scattering of wildflowers, each petal a playful splash of color against a canvas of artistry. Dive into this stitching adventure and let your imagination run wild with every stitch!

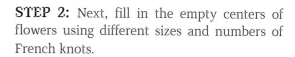

**STEP 1:** Begin by stitching the tops of your florals. For the yellow, pink, and blue flowers, use satin stitch to create your petals of various shapes and sizes. For the peach flower, and the purple flower on the left, use lazy daisy to create your petals. For the purple flower on the top right, create your flower using French knots.

**STEP 2:** Next, fill in the empty centers of flowers using different sizes and numbers of French knots.

**STEP 3:** Stitch your flower stems using back stitch and whipped back stitch. Lastly, use fishbone to stitch all of the leaves.

MATERIALS | **Fabric:** Robert Kaufman Essex Yarn Dyed, Lilac, E064-1191, 55% linen, 45% cotton, 9x9" (22.6x22.6 cm) square
**Thread:** DMC Mouline Six-Strand Cotton, Colors – 30, 164, 210, 369, 433, 520, 562, 604, 725, 727, 961, 967, 976, 3325, 3607
**Needle:** DMC Chenille, size 24
**Equipments:** 7" (18 cm) Beechwood Hoop, Scissors, Heat-erase pen

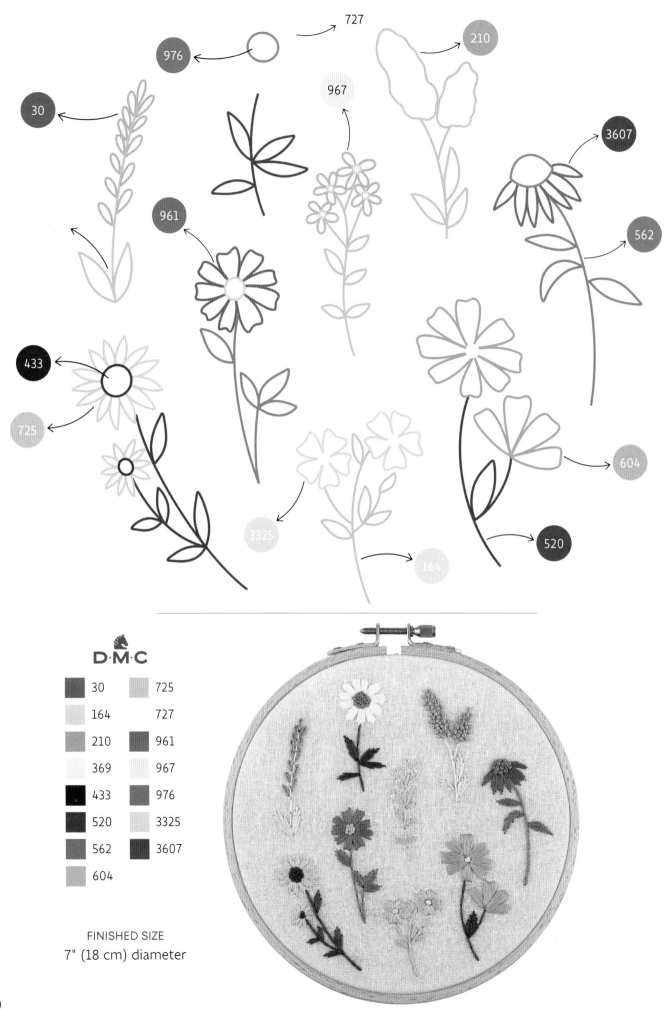

727

976

30

210

967

3607

961

562

433

725

604

3325

520

164

**D·M·C**

| | | | |
|---|---|---|---|
| 30 | | 725 | |
| 164 | | 727 | |
| 210 | | 961 | |
| 369 | | 967 | |
| 433 | | 976 | |
| 520 | | 3325 | |
| 562 | | 3607 | |
| 604 | | | |

FINISHED SIZE
7" (18 cm) diameter

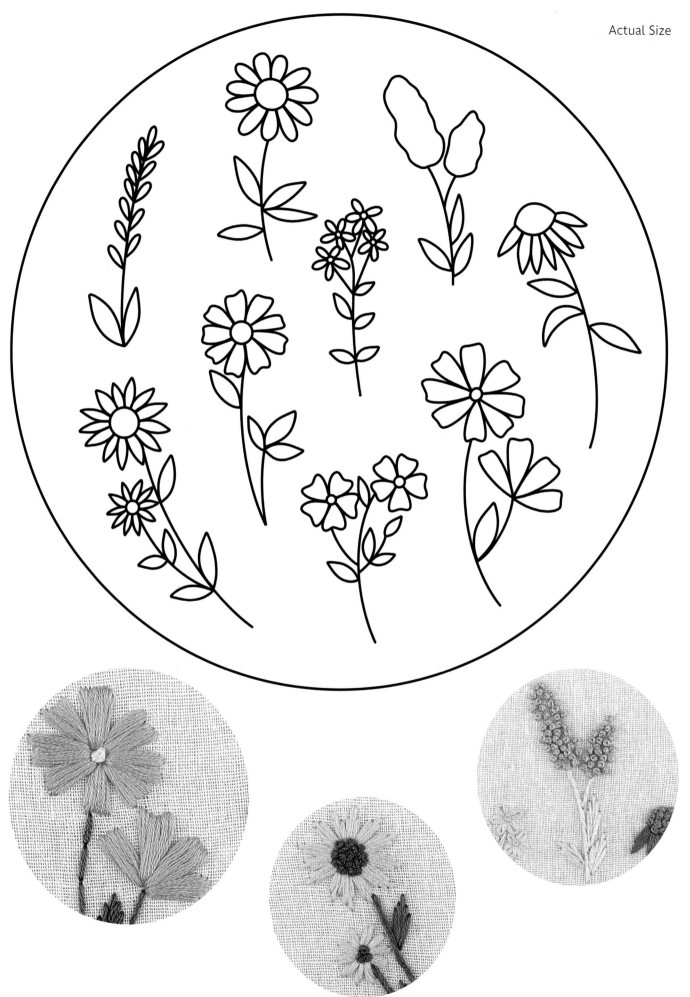

# SPRING *Bicycle*

This piece features a darling pink bicycle adorned with daisy wheels, its baskets brimming with an abundance of colorful flowers. Nestled among the blooms, a puppy adds an extra dose of fun to this delightful scene. Pedal your way into pure joy with every stitch.

**STEP 1:** Begin the piece by stitching the tires. Stitch the circles using three rows of brick stitch in black. The black tire spokes are stitched with simple straight stitches. For the daisies within the tires, stitch the outer petals with whipped back stitch, and the inner petals using a lazy daisy stitch. Fill your center with French knots.

**STEP 2:** Stitch the pink frame of your bicycle using satin stitch, and two rows of brick stitch for the area above the tires. You will also use satin stitch to create the bike seat and handle bars. The pedal area on the bike uses back stitch to create the circle, as well as straight stitches, and satin stitch.

**STEP 3:** Create your baskets using the basket weave stitch, before adding in any other details. Stitch your puppy using satin stitch for the body, head, ear, and paw, and add a tiny French knot for the eye.

**STEP 4:** Finish up your piece by adding your florals blooming from the baskets. Use straight stitches and satin stitch to create the greenery and leaves. Add florals using straight stitches and small woven roses. Scatter some French knots throughout the baskets, and in the centers of your florals to add finishing touches.

MATERIALS | **Fabric:** Kona Cotton, Ice Frappe, K001-1173, 100% cotton, 9x9" (22.6x22.6 cm) square
**Thread:** DMC Mouline Six-Strand Cotton, Colors – 14, 210, 310, 601, 913, 3326, 3342, 3864, Blanc
**Needle:** DMC Chenille, size 24
**Equipments:** 6" (15 cm) Beechwood Hoop, Scissors, Heat-erase pen

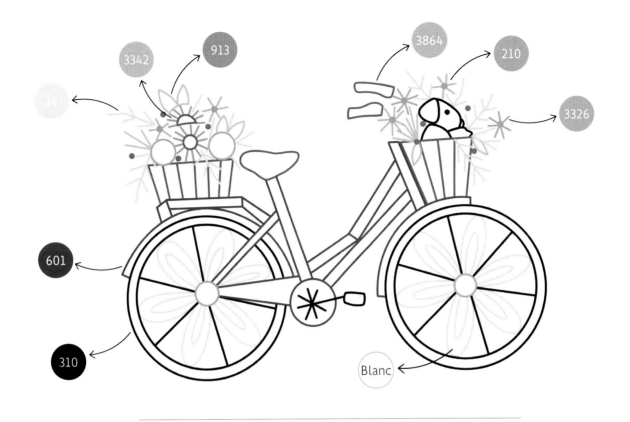

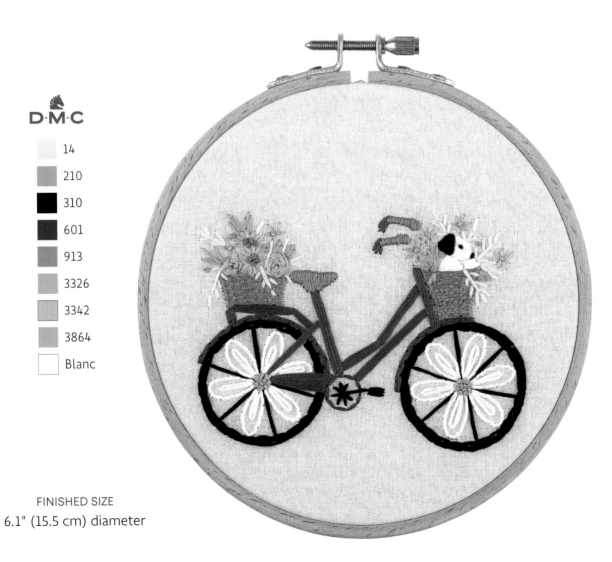

**DMC**

- 14
- 210
- 310
- 601
- 913
- 3326
- 3342
- 3864
- Blanc

FINISHED SIZE
6.1" (15.5 cm) diameter

# FRUITY *Florals*

Stitch up a fruity fiesta featuring a medley of vibrant fruits surrounded by scattered florals, creating a scene of flavor and fun.

**STEP 1:** Your cherries will be stitched using satin stitch. Create the stems using two straight stitches, then stitch your leaves using a fishbone stitch. For your strawberry, you will use rows of chain stitch or reverse chain stitch (personal preference). Stitch your leaves using fishbone. Stitch your citrus fruits and your watermelon by using satin stitch for the skin and inner areas. Use straight stitches to create seeds.

**STEP 2:** For your larger petaled flowers, use a satin stitch for your petals, and fill the centers with French knots. To stitch your roses, use 12-strands of floss and the woven rose stitch. Fill the center of the rose on the right with a few French knots as well.

**STEP 3:** Create your small flowers using the lazy daisy technique. Add finishing touches by scattering some large, white French knots throughout your piece.

MATERIALS | **Fabric:** Kona Cotton, Meringue, K001-1229, 100% cotton, 9x9" (22.6x22.6 cm) square
**Thread:** DMC Mouline Six-Strand Cotton, Colors – 310, 321, 326, 602, 700, 722, 727, 760, 890, 895, 3801, Blanc
**Needle:** DMC Chenille, size 24
**Equipments:** 6" (15 cm) Beechwood Hoop, Scissors, Heat-erase pen

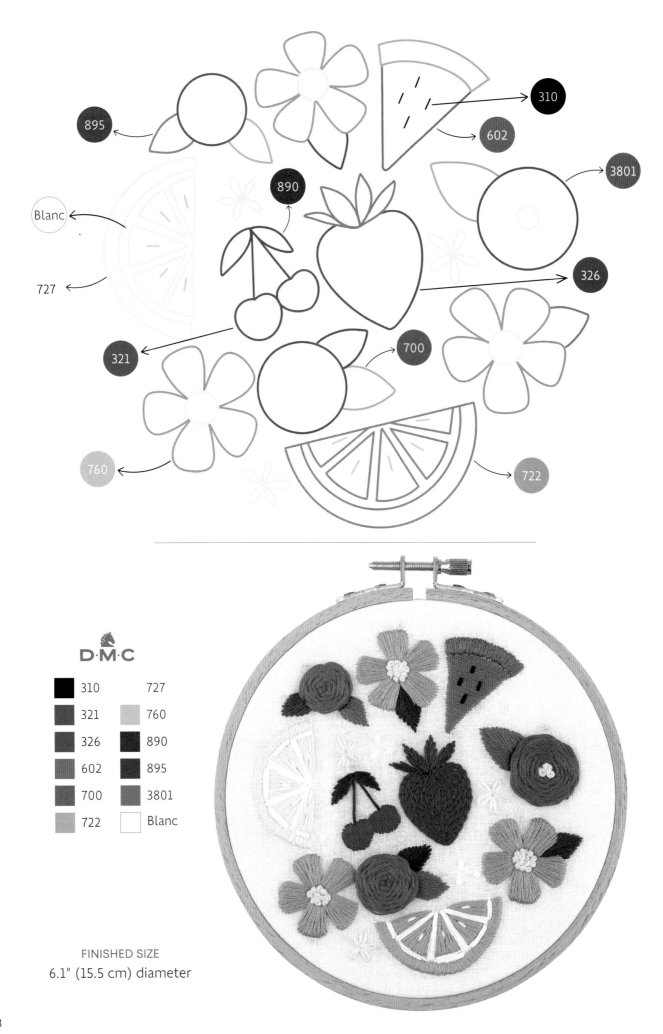

## DMC

| | |
|---|---|
| 310 | 727 |
| 321 | 760 |
| 326 | 890 |
| 602 | 895 |
| 700 | 3801 |
| 722 | Blanc |

FINISHED SIZE
6.1" (15.5 cm) diameter

# SUNNY *Bouquet*

Embroider yourself a little sunshine! This bright bouquet of flowers bursts with color and cheer, and features a radiant sunflower. Let your needle weave beauty as you stitch up this delightful bunch of florals!

**STEP 1:** Start this piece by stitching your three center florals first. Use satin stitch to create your petals, then fill your centers with medium/large French knots.

**STEP 2:** Next, fill in your leafy areas around the flowers using fishbone stitch for a nice leaf texture. Stitch the stems at the top and bottom of the bouquet using a back stitch. Add in the leaves and petals on your tall stems using fishbone and lazy daisy stitches.

**STEP 3:** Add some metallic touches with some lazy daisies around your leaves. Stitch your bow around the bottom stems using two lazy daisies and two straight stitches.

MATERIALS | **Fabric:** Kona Cotton, Butter, K001-1055, 100% cotton, 9x9" (22.6x22.6 cm) square
**Thread:** DMC Mouline Six-Strand Cotton, Colors – 164, 211, 433, 727, 728, 987, 3716, 3805; Metallic Pearl Cotton Size 5, Color - 5283
**Needle:** DMC Chenille, size 24
**Equipments:** 6" (15 cm) Beechwood Hoop, Scissors, Heat-erase pen

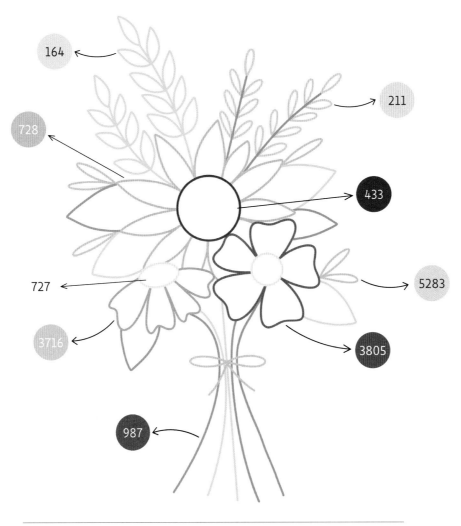

164
211
728
433
727
5283
3716
3805
987

**D·M·C**

| | |
|---|---|
| | 164 |
| | 211 |
| | 433 |
| | 727 |
| | 728 |
| | 987 |
| | 3716 |
| | 3805 |
| | 5283 |

FINISHED SIZE
6.1" (15.5 cm) diameter

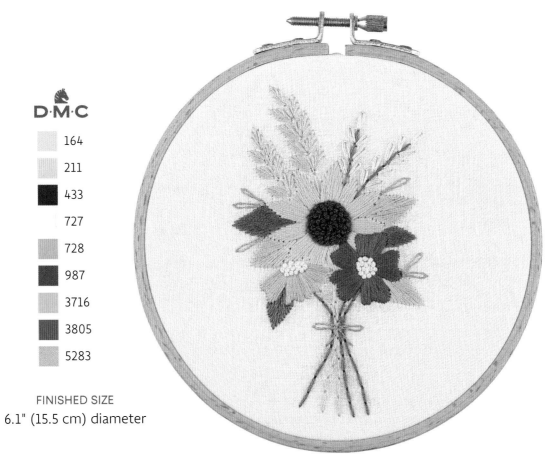

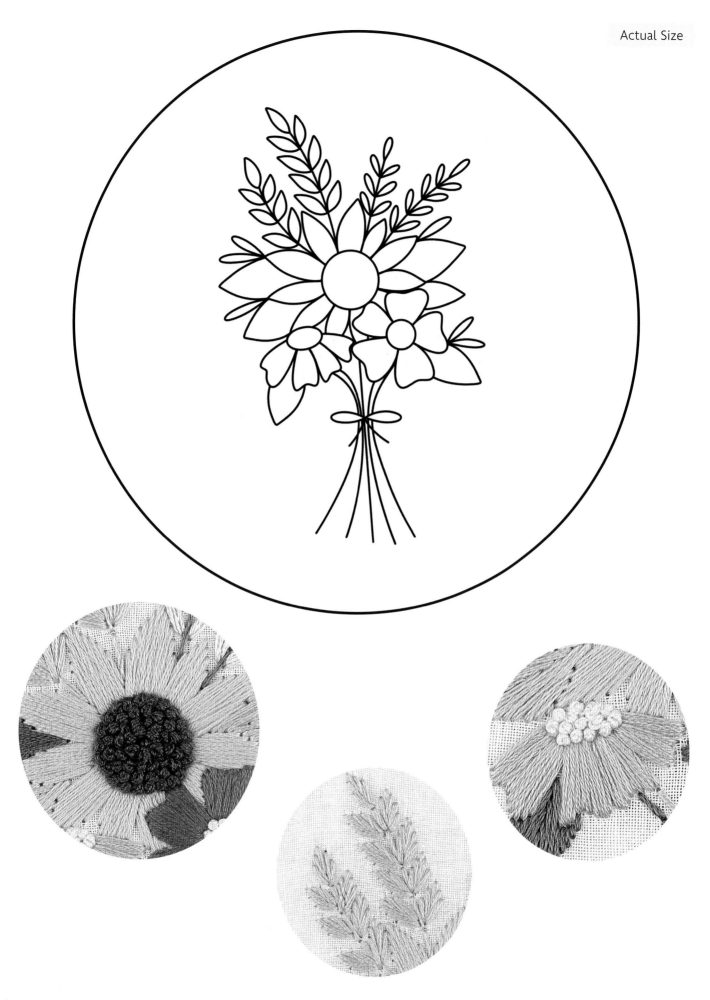

# FRESH *Stems*

Create a bit of springtime mood! This watering can holds a cute bouquet of blossoms, each petal stitched with love. Fluttering around this floral haven are a trio of friends: a sweet ladybug, a graceful butterfly, and a lovely dragonfly.

**STEP 1:** Stitch the watering can outline using a silver metallic thread and a back stitch. At the spout, add four French knots.

**STEP 2:** Stitch your various flowers using satin stitch for your petals, and French knots for the centers. With the poppy, add in some black straight stitch detailing. Next, go in with back stitch to create your stems, and fishbone to add your leaves.

**STEP 3:** Add your garden friends in. For the butterfly and dragonfly, create the bodies and antenna using straight stitches, and lazy daisies for the wings. Your lady bug will be stitched using satin stitch for the wings, with a straight stitch down the center. Add antennas using straight stitches, and French knots for the polka dots.

**MATERIALS | Fabric:** Kona Cotton, Sea Mist, K001-1852, 100% cotton, 9x9" (22.6x22.6 cm) square
**Thread:** DMC Mouline Six-Strand Cotton, Colors −164, 310, 321, 367, 602, 604, 725, 898, 3341; Diamant Grande, Color – G168
**Needle:** DMC Chenille, size 24; DMC Embroidery, size 5
**Equipments:** 6" (15 cm) Beechwood Hoop, Scissors, Heat-erase pen

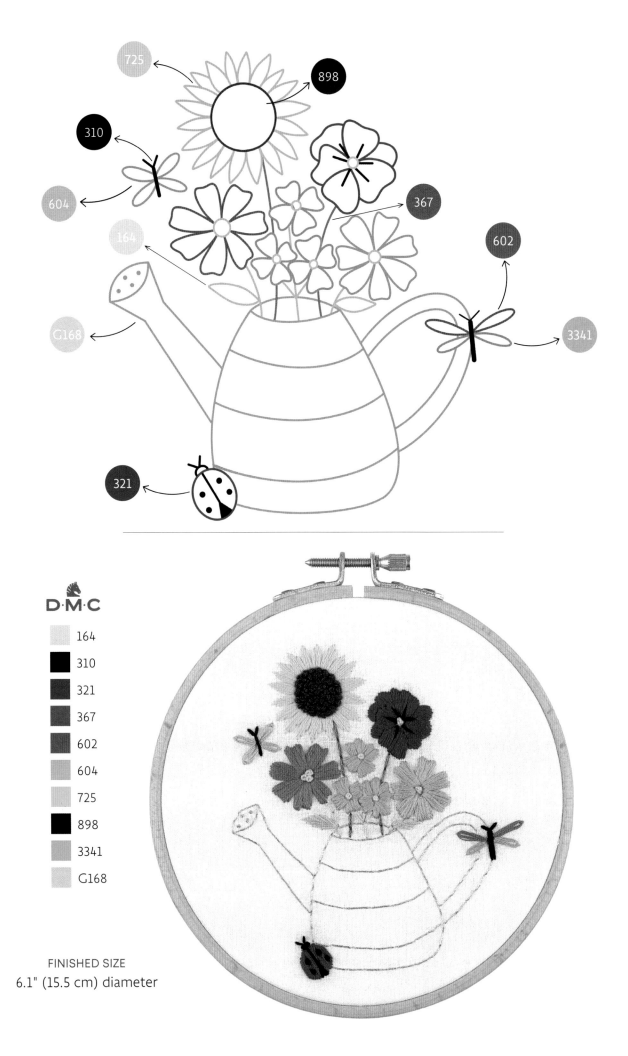

725

898

310

604

367

164

602

G168

3341

321

**D·M·C**

164
310
321
367
602
604
725
898
3341
G168

FINISHED SIZE
6.1" (15.5 cm) diameter

# PERFECT *Posies*

Embrace the subtle beauty of nature with these exquisite posies! Neutral-toned florals take center stage, blossoming with charm. Understated elegance meets playful artistry in this embroidery design.

**STEP 1:** Start by stitching your three and four petaled flowers first, using satin stitch, and adding straight stitch details where needed.

**STEP 2:** Begin to add in your greenery. Stems are stitched using back stitch, and the leaves are stitched using both fishbone and lazy daisy stitches.

**STEP 3:** Fill in the white circular flowers using small French knots.

**STEP 4:** Using 12 strands of thread and the woven rose stitch, carefully create your roses. Fill in the centers of your flowers using French knots. Add scattered French knots throughout the piece for finishing touches.

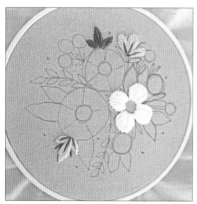  

MATERIALS | **Fabric:** Kona Cotton, Spring, K001-29, 100% cotton, 9x9" (22.6x22.6 cm) square
**Thread:** DMC Mouline Six-Strand Cotton, Colors – 20, 21, 372, 472, 520, 746, 989 3064, 3820, 3852, 3859; Metallic Pearl Cotton Size 5, Color - 5283
**Needle:** DMC Chenille, size 24; DMC Embroidery, size 5
**Equipments:** 5" (13 cm) Beechwood Hoop, Scissors, Heat-erase pen

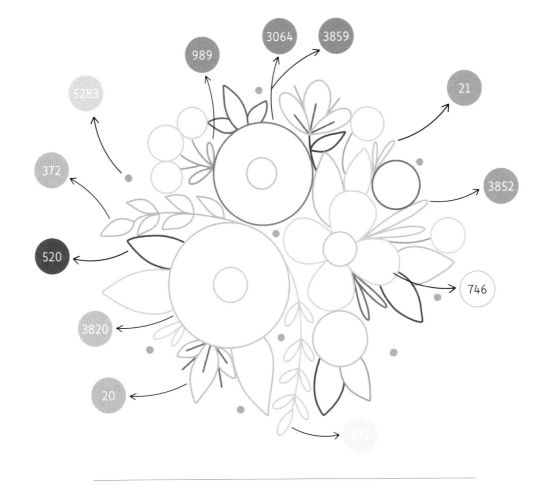

## DMC

| | | | |
|---|---|---|---|
| ▢ | 20 | ▢ | 3820 |
| ▢ | 21 | ▢ | 3852 |
| ▢ | 372 | ▢ | 3859 |
| ▢ | 472 | ▢ | 5283 |
| ▢ | 520 | | |
| ▢ | 746 | | |
| ▢ | 989 | | |
| ▢ | 3064 | | |

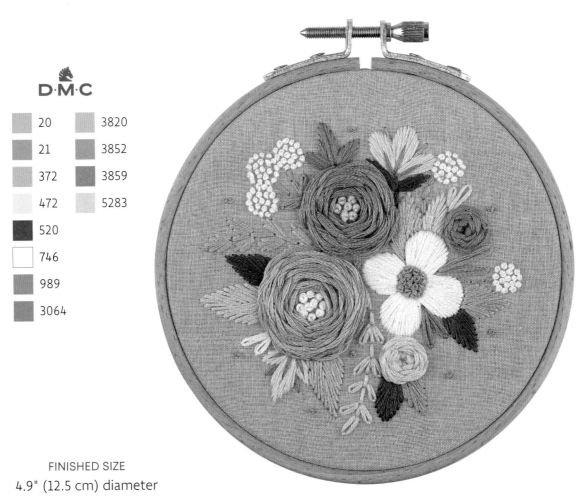

FINISHED SIZE
4.9" (12.5 cm) diameter

# FLOWER *Par-tea*

Enjoy a sip of springtime joy with this sweet design! This quaint teacup is overflowing with pastel florals, each petal stitched with love.

**STEP 1:** Begin by stitching the outline of your teacup using a back stitch. Be sure to leave areas for your leaves and florals that hang over the edges.

**STEP 2:** Stitch your pink, orange, and yellow flowers using satin stitch for the petals. Fill the centers with French knots, and add in your petal details using straight stitches. Stitch the peach flower petals on the upper left using lazy daisy.

**STEP 3:** Add in your greenery by using back stitch for the stems/vines, and fishbone and lazy daisy for the leaves. Stitch your three roses using 12 strands of thread and a woven rose stitch.

**STEP 4:** Stitch your sparkles around the florals using straight stitches, and add in the peach lazy daisy details.

**MATERIALS | Fabric:** Kona Cotton, Snow, K001-1339, 100% cotton, 9x9" (22.6x22.6 cm) square
**Thread:** DMC Mouline Six-Strand Cotton, Colors −19, 164, 211, 353, 727, 955, 957, 964, 3811; Diamant Grande, Color – G168
**Needle:** DMC Chenille, size 24; DMC Embroidery, size 5
**Equipments:** 6" (15 cm) Beechwood Hoop, Scissors, Heat-erase pen

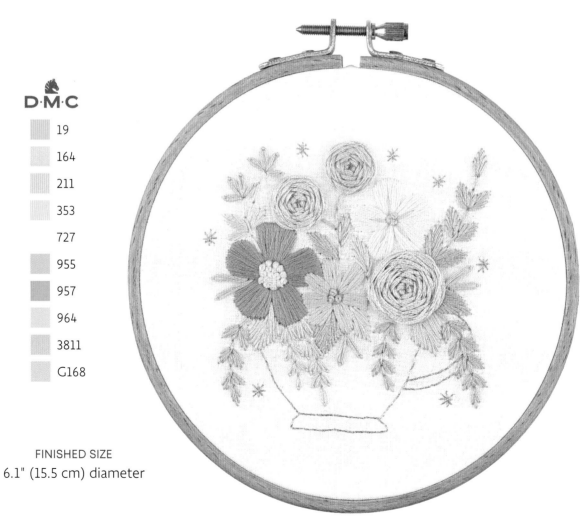

**D·M·C**

- 19
- 164
- 211
- 353
- 727
- 955
- 957
- 964
- 3811
- G168

FINISHED SIZE
6.1" (15.5 cm) diameter

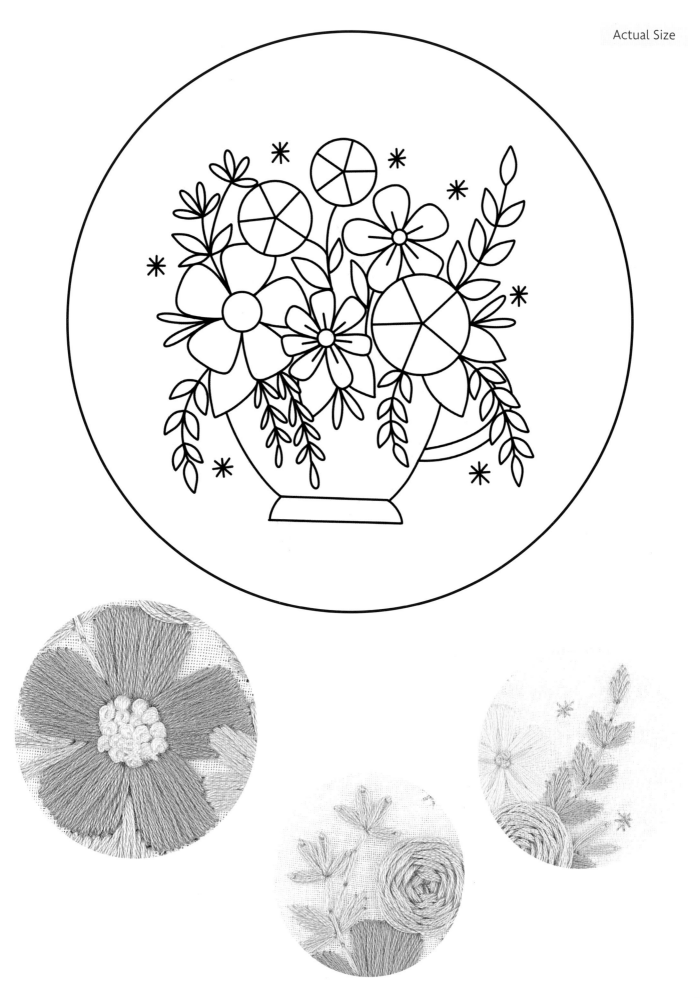

# BLOSSOMING *Love*

Embroider your love for flowers with this heart formed of vibrant blooms. Fill your heart with florals and playful elegance.

**STEP 1:** First, stitch the three 5-petaled flowers using satin stitch for the petals, then fill the centers with French knots.

**STEP 2:** Add in your roses next. Use 12 strands of thread and the woven rose stitch to make them extra fluffy.

**STEP 3:** Lastly, add in your greenery. The stems will be stitched using stem stitch and back stitch. All leaves are stitched using fishbone stitch. You can add in the final touches in yellow using the lazy daisy stitch.

**MATERIALS | Fabric:** Kona Cotton, Peony, K001-110, 100% cotton, 9x9" (22.6x22.6 cm) square
**Thread:** DMC Mouline Six-Strand Cotton, Colors –23, 471, 520, 676, 772, 818, 915, 3804, 3823
**Needle:** DMC Chenille, size 24
**Equipments:** 6" (15 cm) Beechwood Hoop, Scissors, Heat-erase pen

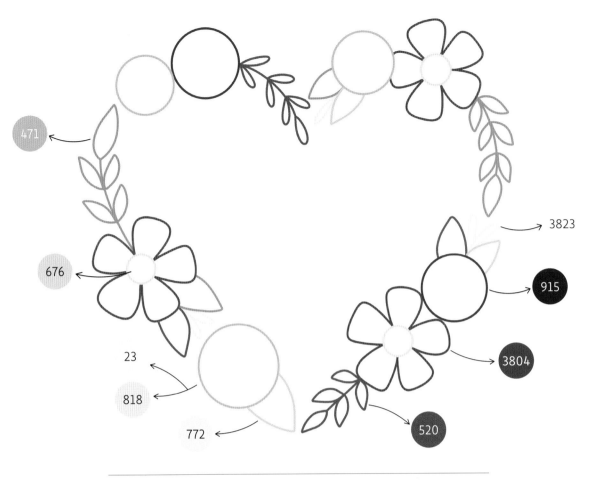

471

3823

676

915

23

3804

818

520

772

**D·M·C**

| | |
|---|---|
| | 23 |
| � | 471 |
| ■ | 520 |
| | 676 |
| | 772 |
| | 818 |
| ■ | 915 |
| ■ | 3804 |
| | 3823 |

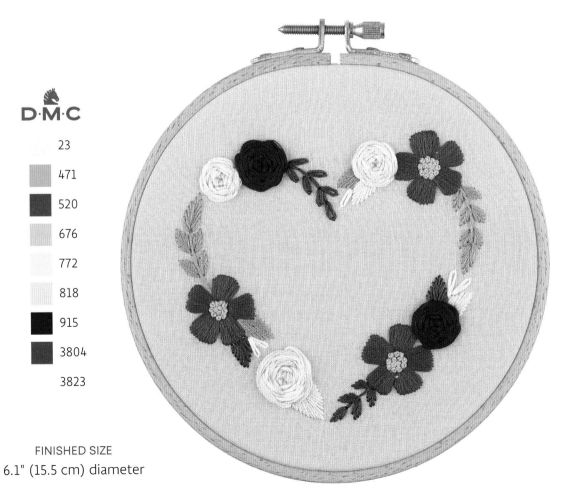

FINISHED SIZE
6.1" (15.5 cm) diameter

# CRESCENT
## Blooms

Escape into a refined scene with this elegant embroidery design - a crescent moon created from a garden of charming flowers, each petal gleaming with delicate sophistication. The silver stars adds a touch of brilliance to the composition.

**STEP 1:** Begin your piece by stitching your petaled flowers using satin stitch. Fill the centers with French knots. Be sure to stay within your outlines to keep the moon shape perfect.

**STEP 2:** Add in your greenery, next. The stems are stitched using back stitch, and the leaves are stitched using fishbone. Add the purple looped petals throughout the piece using the lazy daisy stitch.

**STEP 3:** Stitch your roses with the woven rose stitch. Use 12 strands of floss on your larger roses for a fuller look.

**STEP 4:** Stitch your metallic French knots throughout the moon, and add your straight stitch stars in the center for your finishing touches.

MATERIALS | **Fabric:** Kona Cotton, Peony, K001-110, 100% cotton, 9x9" (22.6x22.6 cm) square
**Thread:** DMC Mouline Six-Strand Cotton, Colors –23, 471, 520, 676, 772, 818, 915, 3804, 3823
**Needle:** DMC Chenille, size 24
**Equipments:** 6" (15 cm) Beechwood Hoop, Scissors, Heat-erase pen

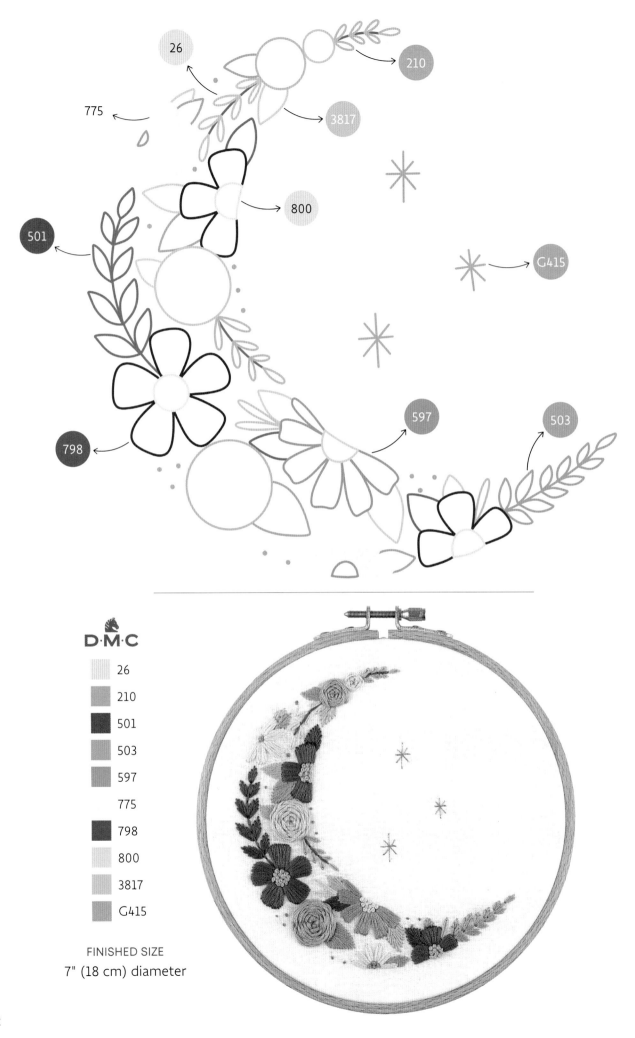

26

210

775

3817

501

800

G415

798

597

503

**DMC**

- 26
- 210
- 501
- 503
- 597
- 775
- 798
- 800
- 3817
- G415

FINISHED SIZE
7" (18 cm) diameter

# RADIANT *Wreath*

Envision your own elegant garden with this radiant floral wreath. This design is brimming with vivid colors and is accented by cascading wisteria that add a touch of charm.

**STEP 1:** First, stitch the five-petal flowers using satin stitch.

**STEP 2:** Begin to stitch your leaves and vines next. For the stems and vines, you will use a back stitch. For all leaves, you will use both fishbone and lazy daisy stitches.

**STEP 3:** Using the woven rose stitch, stitch your roses. For a fuller, fluffy rose, use 12 strands of embroidery floss. Add in your metallic, lazy daisy details around your florals and greenery.

**STEP 4:** Using French knots, fill in the centers of your flowers, as well as the purple florals in the center of your wreath.

MATERIALS | **Fabric:** Kona Cotton, Buttercup, K001-1056, 100% cotton, 9x9" (22.6x22.6 cm) square
**Thread:** DMC Mouline Six-Strand Cotton, Colors –15, 211, 335, 353, 367, 761, 989, 3341, 3823; Metallic Pearl Cotton Size 5, Color - 5283
**Needle:** DMC Chenille, size 24; DMC Embroidery, size 5
**Equipments:** 6" (15 cm) Beechwood Hoop, Scissors, Heat-erase pen

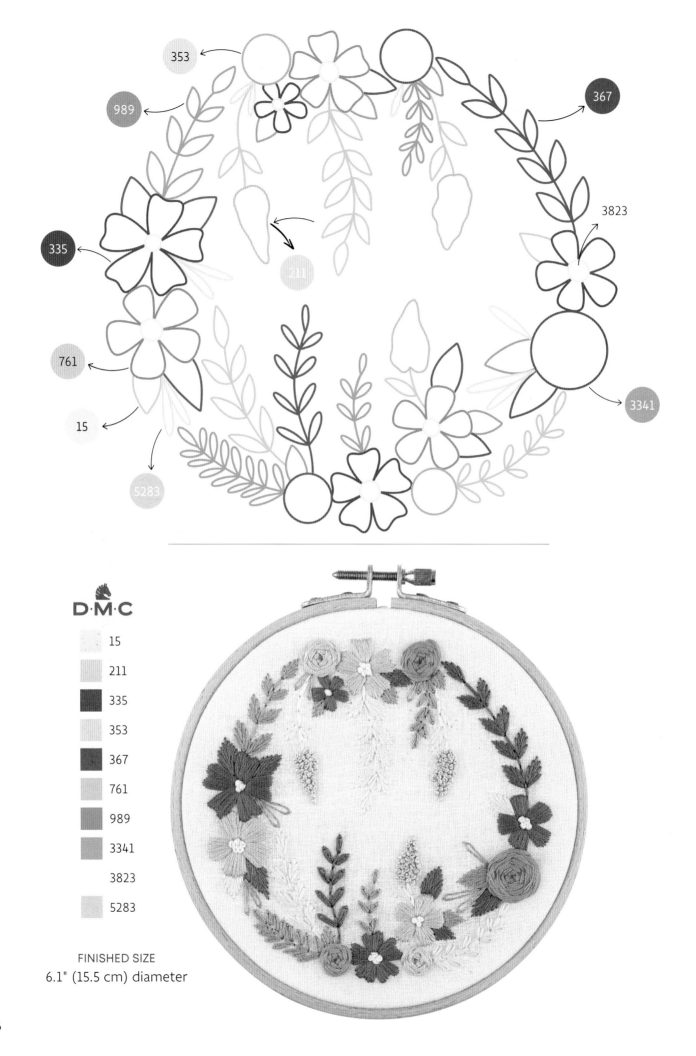

## D·M·C

15
211
335
353
367
761
989
3341
3823
5283

**FINISHED SIZE**
6.1" (15.5 cm) diameter

# FLOATING *Florals*

Embark on a dreamy journey through the skies with this balloon bouquet of vibrant florals. Weave your basket, and float away into a world of floral wonder.

**STEP 1:** Using satin stitch, create your flower petals throughout your "balloon" area. Fill your flower centers with French knots.

**STEP 2:** Stitch your stems and leaves using back stitch and fishbone stitch.

**STEP 3:** Add in your roses using the 12 strands woven rose stitch.

**STEP 4:** Add in the smaller details throughout the balloon area, including the lazy daisy details, French knots, and straight stitch flowers.

**STEP 5:** For the basket rim, use satin stitch across. Stitch your basket using the basket weave stitch from the rim, all the way down to the bottom of the basket. Attach your basket to the "balloon" using four straight stitches.

MATERIALS | **Fabric:** Kona Cotton, Ice Frappe, K001-1173, 100% cotton, 9x9" (22.6x22.6 cm) square
**Thread:** DMC Mouline Six-Strand Cotton, Colors – 26, 151, 369, 436, 502, 554, 917, 3607, 3608, 3817, 3823, 3824
**Needle:** DMC Chenille, size 24
**Equipments:** 6" (15 cm) Beechwood Hoop, Scissors, Heat-erase pen

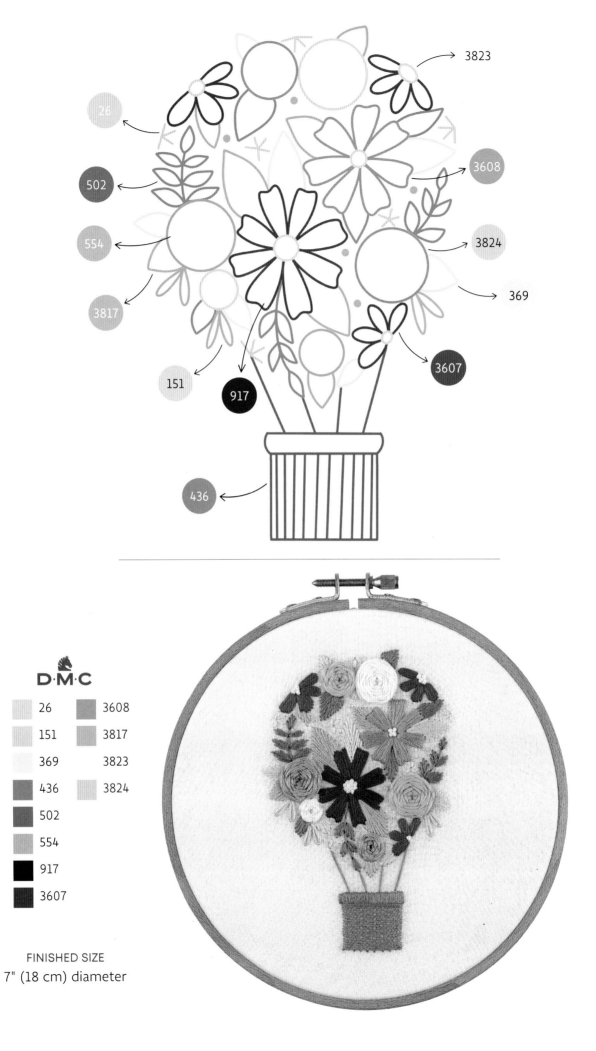

3823

26

502

3608

554

3824

369

3817

151

917

3607

436

**D·M·C**

| | |
|---|---|
| 26 | 3608 |
| 151 | 3817 |
| 369 | 3823 |
| 436 | 3824 |
| 502 | |
| 554 | |
| 917 | |
| 3607 | |

FINISHED SIZE
7" (18 cm) diameter